FINDING BIRDS
on the Great Texas Coastal Birding Trail

NUMBER TWELVE

Gulf Coast Studies

Sponsored by Texas A&M University–Corpus Christi

John W. Tunnell Jr., General Editor

Finding Birds

ON THE GREAT TEXAS COASTAL BIRDING TRAIL

Houston, Galveston,
and the Upper Texas Coast

Ted Lee Eubanks Jr.
Robert A. Behrstock
Seth Davidson

Maps by Cindy Lippincott

TEXAS A&M UNIVERSITY PRESS

COLLEGE STATION

The paper meets the requirements
of ANSI/NISO Z39.48–1992
(Permanence of Paper).
Binding materials have been chosen for durability.

Photographs credited "TLE" are courtesy of Ted Lee Eubanks Jr., and those credited
"RAB/Naturewide Images" are courtesy of Robert A. Behrstock.

On p. i: Blue-headed Vireo, TLE
On the title page: Claybottom Pond, Houston Audubon Society, Smith Oaks Bird
    Sanctuary, High Island, Galveston County (site 53), RAB/Naturewide Images
On p. 19: American White Pelican, TLE

Library of Congress Cataloging-in-Publication Data

Eubanks, Ted.
    Finding birds on the great Texas coastal birding trail : Houston, Galveston, and
the upper Texas coast / Ted Lee Eubanks Jr., Robert A. Behrstock, Seth Davidson ;
maps by Cindy Lippincott. — 1st ed.
        p. cm. — (Gulf Coast studies ; no. 12)
    Includes index.
    ISBN-13: 978-1-58544-534-9 (flexbound : alk. paper)
    ISBN-10: 1-58544-534-7 (flexbound : alk. paper)
        1. Bird watching—Texas—Gulf Coast—Guidebooks.   2. Birds—Texas—
Gulf Coast.   3. Gulf Coast (Tex.)—Guidebooks.   I. Behrstock, Robert A.
II. Davidson, Seth.   III. Title.
    QL684.T4E94   2008
    598.072'347641—dc22   2007028546

Contents

RAB/Naturewide Images

Chestnut-sided Warbler

Birding Tactics

White Ibis

Preface

The purpose of the Great Texas Coastal Birding Trail is to marry the interests of birders, conservationists, and local communities. Funded by the Texas Parks and Wildlife Department and the Texas Department of Transportation, the environmental consulting firm Fermata Inc. assessed hundreds of sites for inclusion on the trail and penned the text for Upper, Central, and Lower Texas Coast maps. This process created a template for additional wildlife watching projects in Texas and other states throughout the nation.

The dream of a route that connects birders to the very best venues that coastal Texas has to offer has in turn fostered more conservation-related projects than even the most expansive thinker could have imagined. The success of the trail convinced Parks and Wildlife to go ahead with another conservation concept—the Great Texas Birding Classic. This annual event, now sponsored by the Gulf Coast Bird Observatory, raises awareness of the important coastal habitats in Texas and generates money for conservation projects. A third ambitious scheme, the World Birding Center in South Texas, also germinated directly from the success of the trails. This project has led a unique coalition of communities, state agencies, and birders to create a system of interpretive centers that jointly serve as a focal point for conservation, tourism, and birding.

The truest measure of success, to say nothing of flattery, is imitation. The birding trails have become a flagship project for conservation in the state of Texas and the scion of a rapidly increasing spawn of other statewide trails. Texas now has a series of trails that cut throughout the state. Florida's statewide birding trail is modeled closely after the pioneering Texas trail. Virginia has also completed a coastal birding trail, and projects in states such as Connecticut, Oregon, Wisconsin, and Oklahoma promise to boost nature-based tourism significantly in all those places. South Africa now has a birding trail in Zululand, patterned exactly after the coastal trail in Texas.

With an estimated 71.1 million Americans watching or feeding wild birds, birding seems to have come into its own. The timing could not be better, because the birds themselves are under tremendous pressure from loss of habitat. Relaxed regulations for development of wetlands, deforestation in Mexico and Central America, urban sprawl here at home, and public policies that suck funds away from conservation have all ratcheted up the pressure on birds and their shrinking habitats. Birders who visit sites on the trail, spending money on gas, food, lodging, equipment, and souvenirs, give communities a direct economic incentive to protect and preserve habitat. Rather than sinking money into other projects such as municipal golf courses or industrial parks, more communities are beginning to get the message of the trail: You can spend minimal funds maintaining and restoring what nature has already provided, while earning maximal tourism revenue from the people who come to visit.

The trail has encouraged communities to restore wetlands, reduce the freshwater pollution of brackish lagoons, develop tourist infrastructure, and pursue habitat management aggressively for the benefit of wildlife. Every person who visits a site on the trail contributes, in ways large and small, to the spread of an environmentalism that turns conservationists and businesses into allies rather than enemies.

An example of such cooperation is Houston's Birds and Bayous, an initiative begun by the Houston Parks and Recreation Department, Houston Audubon Society, Conservation Fund, and Fermata. Birds and Bayous is working to elevate the profile of Houston's remarkable avifauna in the eyes of its residents as well as those who travel there. In the next few years, many of Houston's parks will be enhanced for birders, and certain properties will be managed for their bird diversity.

Development of the trail could never have occurred without the stalwart backing of Andy Sansom, Gary Graham, John Herron, Madge Lindsay, Linda Campbell, and Shelly Plante of the Texas Parks and Wildlife Department. The funding, the prestige they lent to the project, and their total support made the difference between an idle dream and palpable reality. The project's success also depended on the communities, businesspeople, and local birders who jumped at the chance to nominate area sites for inclusion on the trail and who saw this project for what it really was: a golden opportunity to advance conservation and to have fun doing it.

For the resulting book, we are indebted to John Tveten, Gloria Tveten, and Ron Weeks, who carefully reviewed the manuscript and played a crucial role in its development. Shannon Davies and Jennifer Ann Hobson, our editors at Texas A&M University Press, worked tirelessly to make the book a reality.

Of course the tie that binds conservation and business is you, the traveler who enjoys watching wild birds. We thank you for caring enough about wildlife to watch, for caring enough about conservation to spend your travel dollars on a project that supports habitats and the human communities around them, and for sharing our love of wildlife—a love that must be shared in order for the fragile habitats and the wildlife depending on them to survive.

The appearance of high quality, reasonably priced close-focusing binoculars has forever changed our concept of a day in the field. Few Texas birders are now content to concentrate rigidly on birds, and most are just as likely to turn their optics toward a butterfly, a tree frog, or a brightly colored moth. These ancillary observations have been encouraged by a host of new guides to butterflies, dragonflies, mammal, and reptiles, as well as increasingly sophisticated field guides to lesser known fauna such as moths, tiger beetles, and grasshoppers.

The Upper Texas Coast's year-round mild climate and diversity of habitats make it a first class venue for studying all aspects of nature. To that end, we have included photos and discussions of habitats, plants, and animals other than birds in the hope that this book will encourage visitors to immerse themselves in the broader natural history of East Texas, not only its birdlife.

FINDING BIRDS
on the Great Texas Coastal Birding Trail

Wilson's Snipe

RAB/Naturewide Images

Introduction

Pens have run dry expressing high praise for the unbelievable avian diversity found in Texas. Simply put, Texas is the best place in the nation to watch birds. We have the most species, we have the greatest diversity of habitats, and we have spectacle-scale concentrations of avian life. Unlike many other excellent birding venues, coastal Texas goes full-bore for ten months out of the year, and even "quiet" months like January and February can provide dawn-to-dusk action watching a variety of gulls, terns, shorebirds, sparrows, woodpeckers, wintering passerines, and raptors. The mild climate and ideal location of our coastline attract a tremendous variety of other watchable wildlife as well.

For the traveling birder, coastal Texas also offers any number of places to stay and eat—many of our accommodations cater specifically to birders and provide good birding habitat on their grounds. Proximate location to Houston, Galveston, and Beaumont means that travelers can have access to air and ground transportation, to every degree of comfort, and to every type of amenity that they desire. Best of all, nonbirding spouses, friends, and family members will enjoy our beaches, our shopping, and our legendary hospitality.

Finding Birds on the Texas Coast

Texas is undeniably birdy. Yet birders can have great difficulty locating birds that they badly want to see. Books, Web sites, listserves, checklists, and club newsletters provide voluminous

RAB/Naturewide Images

Ted Eubanks at Houston Audubon Society Boy Scout Woods Sanctuary, High Island, Galveston County (SITE 55)

RAB/Naturewide Images

American Lady

data on where the birds are. For the avid birder, equipped with decades of experience and the best optical equipment, these resources work admirably.

For most birders, however, knowing where the birds are is a separate issue from knowing how to find them onsite. Most people who watch and feed birds cannot distinguish a dozen sparrow species at a glance, cannot identify every warbler by its song, and cannot pick out the handful of Ross's Geese amid a thousand-strong flock of migrating Snow Geese. For many birders, simply knowing where expert birders go to find birds is not enough. Why? Because finding birds is affected by season, weather, time of day, the behavioral idiosyncracies of each species, and the tactics employed by the birder.

Over the lifetime of this trail, which hosts an estimated 250,000 visitors per year, we have often heard that "there weren't any birds" at a particular site. In many situations we believe that to have been the case. In many others, though, the birds were in fact there, but the visitor did not know how to find them. Without birds to look at or listen to, the threshold activity in birding—"What bird is this?"—never comes into play, and the traveler moves on to the next site somewhat disappointed or, worse, gives up the endeavor altogether.

This guidebook tells you where the birds are *and* how to find them. For the experienced birder, it provides the traditional detailed information about which sites host which target birds. For the casual and less experienced birder, it provides tactics for finding certain groups of birds as the trail progresses through various venues, as well as tactics that birders can use at a given site to find specific birds. These tactics include a range of tools gleaned from decades of experience birding the Texas coast, tools that any birder of any level can immediately use to *find the birds*.

We hope this guidebook takes you beyond travel directions and species lists and into the realm of making the birds come to you, enabling you to view the greatest diversity of birds along this incomparably rich coastline and to delve into the sublime appeal of birding: watching wild things in their natural state, giving names to the things we see, and feeling like a participant in the great mysteries of the natural world.

Habitat Strategy

Geography defines evolution. Birders, in varying degrees, implicitly understand that it defines the occurrence of birds as well. Who would look for an albatross in the Colorado Rockies? The Texas coast is no exception:

noticing geographic peculiarities and the plant and animal communities associated with them is the surest starting point for getting on the bird.

Ideally, the birder is a world-class botanist, marine biologist, mammal expert, entomologist, and infallible weather forecaster all rolled into one. Practically speaking, a very rough knowledge of habitats and which birds associate with them suffices to increase greatly the number of birds that will pop into view. At its most basic level, such habitat awareness means the traveler need only note that different coastal venues have different vegetation of varying shape and height. The probability that a given bird will occur at a given place is primarily driven by habitat. Once the birder identifies the habitat, the number of possible birds becomes significantly narrower as well.

The broad habitat types on the trail are finite: woodlands, prairies, wetlands, water surfaces, edge, and sky. Visitors who concentrate on the physical structure of each site, and categorize it as one of the six main groups, will have a much better chance of *seeing expected birds* than visitors who simply show up and wait for any of Texas' more than six hundred bird species to appear. Progressing along the trail will also take travelers to a variety of habitats that are subcategories of the major ones listed. Since different birds have different needs for food and cover, these subcategories indicate that a different coterie of birds may be present. Much more important, they also indicate which birds will likely not be present. Birding by elimination is what habitat recognition is all about.

WOODLANDS

The woodland habitat subcategories on the Texas coast tend to be:

Hardwood: The deciduous trees making up this kind of woodland have leaves that change color in fall and then drop off. Primarily found in East Texas, they attract a variety of warblers, tanagers, and woodpeckers.

Pine/oak: Pine is found primarily in the Big Thicket and Trinity loops of the Great Texas Coastal Birding Trail. Oak occurs sporadically throughout the rest of the trail. It is particularly important as a shelter and food source for coastal migrants. Check clumps of oaks, or mottes, during fall and spring migration.

Wet: Woodlands that have a flooded or damp understory (Bear Creek Park, Harper's Church Road) can attract specialty birds such as Rusty Blackbird.

Dry: Dry pine woodlands in East Texas provide habitat for a variety of warblers and woodpeckers. Dry scrub woodlands attract flycatchers and other kingbirds.

Coastal: During spring groundings or fall massings, coastal woodlands can attract huge

RAB/Naturewide Images

Six-lined Racerunner

concentrations of passerines (song birds). Stands at High Island, Sabine Woods, Quintana Neotropical Bird Sanctuary, and Galveston Island State Park (sites 52–55, 26, 121, and 70) can be migrant magnets.

Inland: In winter, inland forests and thickets can host large feeding flocks of insectivores—birds that eat insects. Inland forests are prime habitat for breeding warblers and tanagers in late spring and summer. Visit Martin Dies Jr. State Park, Gore Store Road and Turkey Creek, Armand Bayou Nature Center, and Dow Centennial Bottomlands Park (sites 13, 16, 81, and 114).

Urban: Mature artificial woodlands in city parks and neighborhoods can concentrate large numbers of birds during all seasons. Mature exotic urban plantings can also provide significant wintering habitat for hummingbirds.

Scrub: Scraggly, sparse, brushy trees interspersed with prairie or pasture make up this woodland subcategory. Little of this habitat remains; what is left is primarily in Waller County, where huisache scrub attracts eastern Bewick's Wren, Palm Warbler, and flycatchers and marks the easternmost range of the Ladder-backed Woodpecker.

Isolated stands: Clumps of trees

Waller County

on prairie and roadside hedges and thickets attract feeding flocks of insect-eating birds and wintering sparrows.

Creekside/riverside: Riparian woodlands attract owls, warblers, tanagers, flycatchers, and woodpeckers.

PRAIRIES

These fall into two types:

Inland: These open areas can be agricultural fields or stands of native grass. The Katy Prairie (site 99) is the best representative and attracts wintering sparrows, shorebirds such as Long-billed Curlew, geese, and a wide variety of raptors.

Coastal: Wet grassland that is periodically inundated makes up this kind of prairie. Saltmeadow cordgrass (*Spartina patens*) is a salt-tolerant coastal prairie species

Katy Prairie

indicative of this habitat type. This is the primary wintering habitat for Sedge Wren and Yellow Rail.

WETLANDS

Our varied wetland habitats include:

Coastal freshwater: The most productive coastal freshwater wetlands are flooded rice fields, which attract a wide variety of shorebirds during migration.

Coastal saltwater: Several specialty sparrows and rails occur in this type of habitat.

Coastal brackish: The level of salinity can be identified by various sedges, *Spartina,* and *Phragmites.* Look for yet another coterie of birds here.

Coastal mudflat: Ideal shorebird habitat, mudflats are good for skimmers, gulls, plovers, and terns. Bolivar Flats and San Luis Pass (sites 58 and 71) typify this habitat.

Coastal beach: Shoreline habitat, as at Galveston Island State Park and Surfside, attracts Sanderlings, Ruddy Turnstones, gulls, and terns.

Inland mudflat: Often associated with ponds that have dried up, or with small bodies of water that have muddy edges, such habitat attracts shorebirds including plovers and snipe.

Caspian Terns

RAB/Naturewide Images

Snow Geese

Inland freshwater: Marshy areas and flooded fields attract ibis, ducks, grebes, and associated raptors.

WATER SURFACES

These can be *fresh water*, attracting dabbling ducks, grebes, and raptors; *bay waters*, attracting pelicans and mergansers; or *nearshore waters*, which attract gannets. Diving ducks favor all three kinds of water surfaces.

EDGE

Edge means the confluence of different habitat types and can be extremely productive for both numbers of birds and diversity of species. Look for places where woodland meets prairie, where mudflats become marshy, or where freshwater ponds are juxtaposed with wooded thickets or grassy areas.

SKY

Several of the Upper Texas Coast's most striking avian phenomena occur overhead. Occasionally, such birds are present in large, noisy, and easily seen flocks. Other species are silent, but the experienced observer will glance upward periodically so as not to miss their presence.

The most widely recognized local bird movement is the fall migration of white geese. During October and November, huge flocks of Snow and Ross's geese arrive from their nesting grounds on Hudson Bay. Preceding the white geese are flocks of noisy White-fronted Geese and, especially inland, Canada Geese alert us to their presence with their familiar honking.

Our most visible and spectacular daytime migration of songbirds is that of swallows (see San Luis Pass, site 71).

Hawk watching has become a popular birding pastime, especially the fall Hawk Watch at Candy Ab-shier Wildlife Management Area or WMA (site 48). During favorable conditions, day after day, hundreds to hundreds of thousands of birds of prey, often in kettles—huge swirling and climbing spires—pass by on their journeys to warmer climes. With few exceptions, these kites, buteos, ac-cipiters, and falcons appear silently, occasionally at treetop level but, as the morning's thermals develop, they are more likely to be seen high over-head. Among them may be dozens to thousands of equally quiet Anhingas, Wood Storks, and White Pelicans, in numbers far surpassing what we'd expect to see if searching for these birds on the ground.

Two final notes on habitat: the more types you visit, the more species you will see. When pressed for time, focus on sites that offer different habitat se-lections. Most important, remember that bird habitat is not limited to the sites on the trail map. In the rush to reach High Island, birders can easily overlook a rarity along the roadside—nestled in a promising habitat waiting to be *pisshed* up. Watch for changes in vegetation, and keep in mind that if the habitat is right, it could well be worth stopping for a look.

RAB/Naturewide Images

Black Skimmer

Seasonal Strategy

Subordinate to habitat is season. Certain birds and certain birding phenomena occur at certain times of the year. Although a bird may be present for many months, behavior that allows it to be seen may occur for only a few weeks. Finding wood warblers in the dense canopy of the Big Thicket is much easier in late spring and early summer because the males have staked out territory and are defending it with song—vocalizations that cue the viewer to the bird's otherwise inconspicuous location. Later in the summer, when the chorus has concluded, finding these same birds may be virtually impossible.

By the same token, so much bird behavior and occurrence is related to seasonal timing that many birders are overwhelmed with the detail. Here are some general seasonal brushstrokes for locating birds on the Upper Texas Coast:

1. Look for migrating vireos, warblers, buntings, and tanagers on the coast from mid- to late spring.

2. Look for many of these same warblers inland from late spring to early summer.

3. Look for *Empidonax* flycatchers on the coast in fall.

4. Look for sparrows in winter.

5. Look for hummingbirds in winter. While they are most com-

mon by far in fall (they winter in a fraction of the fall numbers), species diversity is much greater in winter.

6. Look for shorebirds, woodpeckers, and owls year-round.

7. Look for raptors in winter.

Seasonal birding on the Upper Texas Coast offers incredible rewards. As an example, there is a greater diversity of shorebirds here in spring than virtually anywhere in North America. By working coastal habitats from about April 15 through May 7, you can see thirty-six species in a day; thirty-seven if you have the time to search inland for American Woodcock. The key to spring shorebirding is diverse habitats: rice fields and freshwater ponds in Brazoria and Chambers counties as well as saltwater habitat at Bolivar Flats, East Beach, and San Luis Pass must all be checked. Here is what is possible:

SALTWATER
Black-bellied Plover
Snowy Plover
Wilson's Plover
Piping Plover
American Oystercatcher
American Avocet
Willet
Marbled Godwit
Red Knot
Sanderling
Short-billed Dowitcher

RAB/Naturewide Images

American Oystercatcher

FRESHWATER
American Golden-Plover
Killdeer
Black-necked Stilt
Greater Yellowlegs
Lesser Yellowlegs
Solitary Sandpiper
Spotted Sandpiper
Upland Sandpiper
Whimbrel
Hudsonian Godwit
Semipalmated Sandpiper
Least Sandpiper
White-rumped Sandpiper
Baird's Sandpiper
Pectoral Sandpiper
Stilt Sandpiper
Buff-breasted Sandpiper
Long-billed Dowitcher
Wilson's Snipe
Wilson's Phalarope
BOTH
Semipalmated Plover
Long-billed Curlew

Ruddy Turnstone
Western Sandpiper
Dunlin

Groundings

Thousands of birders flock to the Texas coast every spring hoping to witness a fallout. Virtually all are disappointed in this expectation, however much fun they may have witnessing the colorful, dynamic spectacle of even an average spring day at High Island.

The reason few people witness fallouts, or groundings, is surprisingly simple: timing is everything. The majority of the birds that winter south of Texas return in the spring by flying directly across the Gulf of Mexico. In conditions favorable for them, southeast winds and clear skies make this flight so uneventful that most of the birds continue far inland and avoid the upper coast altogether. Fallouts require a late cold front with strong winds and rain: these are the conditions that force tens of thousands of migrating birds to the ground. These fallouts are among the most spectacular wildlife dramas on earth, when every bush is alive with exhausted warblers, tanagers, and grosbeaks.

If you miss the cold front, you miss the fallout. It's that simple. Birders intent on experiencing these rare events must chase the cold fronts. Watch the Weather Channel for a late-season front that stalls along the coast with strong north winds and rain, then head for Sabine Woods, High Island, Bolivar Peninsula, Quintana, and Galveston. This is not a pursuit for those with steady jobs or needy dependents.

Massings

Interestingly enough, the same phenomenon that concentrates birds exists in the fall, yet most birders are oblivious to it. In fall, migrants surf southward, taking advantage of trailing northerly winds from the first cold fronts. These pushes, or waves of fall migrants, provide birding opportunities equal to those of the spring. Since fall fronts are surfed by birds that winter here as well as by those that migrate farther south, on

occasion a large number of species that would normally stop to winter in the woodlands of East Texas are blown south or southeast to the coast. Brown Creepers on beachside telephone poles, Red-breasted Nuthatches, Common Ground-Doves, and clouds of Pine Siskins feeding in the grassy beach dunes, Cassin's Sparrows at the end of a jetty—all of these anomalies happen when weather conditions conspire with bird movements.

As in spring, watch for the first strong fronts that blow all the way to the coast, because they will clean out good numbers of birds that have been waiting for a tailwind. After the cold front brings the birds to the coast, the prevailing wind almost always becomes southeasterly, a headwind, which causes the new arrivals to pile up and stage as they await the next tailwind. Hawks, geese, Anhingas—everything going south surfs these fronts. In sum, during times of dramatic weather changes in spring and fall, be on the coast.

Listen, Then Look

Birding strategies can be plotted on a continuum ranging from little effort to extraordinary effort. Some birders get ample satisfaction gazing out at the feeder in the yard—particularly if the feeder is in Ecuador, and the yard list is five hundred birds strong. Others make it a vocation and spare no resource in the quest to see and identify as many birds as possible. It's easy to argue about the relative merits of different strategies, but one statement seems pretty safe: the more attention you pay to bird sounds, the more birds you will see. The corollary to this truism is that birding by ear can be the most effective strategy for finding birds once in habitat.

This is where many birders throw up their hands. Listening to bird song is daunting, and becoming a master of avian vocalizations is a lifelong endeavor. For the many birders who have purchased expensive bird song CDs and given up in frustration, for those who have simply concluded that they cannot discriminate be-tween vocalizations, and for those who have yet to incorporate listening into their arsenal, we offer some straightforward advice for birding by ear on the Texas coast.

First, the good news: effective listening requires zero ability to identify bird songs. It requires simply that you register noise when you hear it and follow the noise until you can get your glasses on the bird that is making it: *Listen, then look.* Birds can be terribly noisy creatures, and even the birder who cannot identify a howling mob of jays by sound will likely be led by the racket to the jays and to the owl that they are harassing. That makes two bird sightings from one simple act of listening.

Second, the better news: listening for bird sounds, as opposed to identifying bird song, can be significantly improved with minimal effort. We learn to screen out sound in urban environments and can block out loud sounds such as the hum of the refrigerator, the roar of rush hour traffic, and countless other auditory intrusions. How much more easily do we block out smaller and subtler ones! Most urbanites have simply forgotten how to hear sounds in nature. The recognition of natural noise in habitat constitutes 90 percent of bird finding wherever concealment is a major avian survival strategy—that is to say, in woods, thickets, grasslands, and marshes.

RAB/Naturewide Images

Hermit Thrush

Third, on the Upper Texas Coast, listening for bird song is generally a factor only in the late spring and early summer. After the wood warblers have stopped singing on territory, the critical sound in forests and thickets, grasslands and marshes, is bird *noise*. It could be rustling in the leaf litter, contact notes and chips between members of a feeding flock, or a hammering bill on the bole of a tree. These and other noises are cues that can lead you to the birds, regardless of whether you can identify the species by the sound of its chip.

For the birder who does not want to use tapes, auditory cues are often the only way to get on the bird. In many cases, they may also be the only way to make a positive identification. Birders and their books tend to make distinctions between field marks and vocalizations, but in reality the two are interdependent. A cue is a cue, and the birder who wants to see more birds and then identify them will tap into this first set of auditory cues in order to decipher the visual ones, even if deciphering means nothing more than "look in the direction of the sound."

It is this sensitivity to bird sound, this finding-by-ear approach, that draws birders into the realm of identification by ear. Once you are attuned to every backyard auditory cue, the titmouse, chickadee, cardinal, grackle, Downy Woodpecker, House Wren, House Sparrow, and fox squir-rel become background noise that the mind can instinctively interpret, just as you can hear the car engine without listening to it. In the same way that the engine's sound intrudes into consciousness only when it starts to run strangely, forcing your ear to acknowledge all the backyard sounds will eventually cause those nonyard sounds to stand out. If grackles and House Sparrows are the background noise, Hermit Thrush will stand out.

Auditory birding can be especially effective at night. Migrants are often quite vocal, especially as they cross over Galveston at low altitudes. In spring you can hear the flutelike whistles of Upland Sandpiper, Dickcissel, *Catharus* thrushes, and Indigo Bunting on nights of heavy migratory movement, particularly when inclement weather keeps the birds flying low. The cacophony of sounds produced on a good night in spring or fall, as well as the songs of Chuck-will's-widow and Eastern Screech-Owl, become part of the Texas birding experience in direct proportion to one's attentiveness to sound.

Constraints of time and money also argue for birding by ear on the Texas coast. The physical area is vast, the number of trail sites is large, and travelers can waste significant time at sites that have little or no bird activity. Driving to a site, listening for a feeding flock, and moving on if the area seems silent embody our concept that, for the most part, birding on the upper coast should be done from sound to sound, not from site to site. The ear should steer. No matter how much or how little a birder becomes immersed in mastering bird sounds, the simple act of *listen, then look* will reap great rewards on the trail.

All that said, there are still people for whom listening is simply too much bother. That is okay, too. There is still much to enjoy, not the least of which are our many shorebirds, gulls, terns, and raptors, for which vocalizations are less important for finding and identifying than are visual cues.

To Call or Not to Call

Birders tend to come down hard on one side or the other of the debate about calling: attracting birds with squeaks, whistles, and playback tapes is either acceptable or despicable. The fact is that if you can get to the habitat, calling up birds by whatever method will produce more sightings than strolling quietly in the woods— although it may not produce more birds than sitting quietly in a blind. Expert birders almost invariably utilize some combination of call-up techniques. Unfortunately, excessive disturbance can harm the bird and can turn nature viewing into an artificial, "staged" experience. Drawing the line between minor and excessive

disturbance is difficult to do, not least because for many species we do not know the effect that repeated tape playback may have.

Calling up birds in protected areas or amid threatened populations is plainly wrong. Calling up birds where it disturbs their nesting activities is just as bad. Calling up birds where it interferes with other birders or where it constitutes an unwanted aesthetic intrusion seems equally unreasonable. Throwing rocks into a marsh to scare up a rail is particularly objectionable. Yet we personally believe that the advantages of calling techniques used judiciously and in moderation outweigh the risk of disturbing the birds. If this seems self-serving, it bears remembering that the greatest threat to avian diversity is not a few squeaky owl imitations, or even hunters who shoot birds out of the sky, but the wholesale loss of habitat due to development: there are more meaningful stands to make in the world of conservation than a do-or-die rejection of calling up birds. Moreover, we are firmly convinced that birding is more enjoyable when there are birds to see. If we could call up butterflies and dragonflies, we would probably do that too—in moderation.

We do most of our bird calling by creating the impression that there is a predator present. Birds have remarkable responses to outside stimuli. They need to see and are most vulnerable when their vision is obstructed. Therefore an owl, or a small flock of birds scolding an owl, either of which can be imitated by a birder, will often attract birds that come over to locate, identify, scold, or drive off the predator.

Calling up birds is seasonal and species-specific: it works best on the Upper Texas Coast in winter with woodland birds and sparrows. When you are in habitat, listen carefully for the sounds of any bird activity. Calling up birds in an empty thicket will produce a whole lot of nothing—what respectable actor presents a play to an empty theater? Once you hear a chirp or click, you may have located a feeding flock. Your job is now to convince the birds that a predator has arrived.

RAB/Naturewide Images

Green Treefrog

First, do a low whistle. If you try to gargle at the same time, which simply involves vibrating your epiglottis with the flow of air (practice, practice), you will produce a reasonable imitation of an Eastern Screech-Owl. Next, make a loud *pissh* sound. This imitates the scolding of a wren—in this little drama, the predator calls, the defending bird scolds, and for the coup de grâce a squeaking sound is made by sucking against the back of the hand. The piteous victim has been grasped by the evil owl and emits a pathetic squeak as it expires.

Wildlife impromptu! This call-scold-squeak sequence is most productive when one of the typical scolding woodland birds such as a titmouse, chickadee, gnatcatcher, or wren joins in the warning chorus. When one of these birds begins chattering, you have got it made—any other birds in the feeding flock will race to the edge to see what is going on. A particularly good imitation may cause a real screech-owl to join in, confirming that the birds have been taken in by the drama. Yet beware: a Barn Owl or Great Horned Owl may respond to this as well, and a swoop from one of these large predators can be startling.

RAB/Naturewide Images

Water Lily

Couch Potato Birding

Despite our espousal of proactive methods for locating birds, it is often preferable simply to pick a vantage point and subordinate the viewing experience to the rhythm of nature. Blending in and letting the birds come to you is an excellent strategy for viewing some of the trails, for spring warblers at Purkey's Pond, for hawk watches at Smith Point, and for loon and waterfowl scoping at Offatt's Bayou. Another powerful strategy is to sit or stand on the edge of a tidal mudflat during a rising tide, watching while the approaching water slowly pushes thousands of feeding shorebirds toward your dry vantage point. Mobility impairment, excessive heat and humidity, or the desire to observe extended bird behavior rather than simply check off species are all situations that call for blending in.

The best expression of this approach is a blind. Commercially available portable blinds allow you to disappear from the landscape, but the same effect can often be achieved by sitting quietly in the car, on a bench, or at a feeder.

Rating the Sites

The Upper Texas Coast portion of the Great Texas Coastal Birding Trail has more than 120 sites, usually marked by a brown and white Great Texas Coastal Birding Trail sign. When time and money are factors, and they always seem to be, it is difficult to visit every site. Moreover, depending on the time of year, the time of day, and what the visitor seeks, at some sites the probability of a rich birding experience is close to zero. On the other hand there are the heavyweight venues that promise plenty of watchable wildlife, at the very least, and a birding bonanza when firing on all cylinders.

Over the lifespan of the trail we have fielded numerous queries about which sites are the best. This question is as dismaying as when the sommelier is asked to recommend "the best wine." Lacking a foolproof methodology for divining the needs and expectations of every birder in coastal Texas, yet recognizing a need for some general guidance, we decided to wing it. Sites at which we have seen lots of great birds over a spectrum of seasons and weather conditions we rated with a three. Sites where the potential is limited to the favorable confluence of habitat, season, weather phenomena, and a small number of widespread birds we rated with a one. Sites that fall somewhere in between we rated with a two.

This gestalt approach leaves much to be desired—we accept in advance all criticism of this nonscientific, arbitrary rating system, and we grant the validity of the critique on all counts. At the same time this system represents the judgment of enthusiastic birders who have spent considerable time at many of these venues, a judgment that we hope visitors will find preferable to no guidance at all. We hope visitors who do not yet have a working knowledge of this vast and diverse geographic area will be able to follow these generalized ratings in order to have the greatest number of gratifying wildlife experiences in the shortest amount of time. We want to emphasize, however, that a site with a low rating can still offer up the most treasured sighting of the trip, particularly when habitat, season, weather, and species are all invoked for deciding whether to visit the site.

After the first draft of this text was prepared, Hurricane Rita swept across many of the trail's easternmost sites. In some cases—for example, Sabine Woods (site 26)—damage was minimal. In others, including several sites in the Big Thicket region, tree damage was widespread. Invariably, such damage encourages salvage logging, often in the form of clear-cuts. During early 2006, we revisited many sites to assess the hurricane's impact on them. While most sites retain populations of their characteristic birds, certain species may be more difficult to find.

Birding the Trail

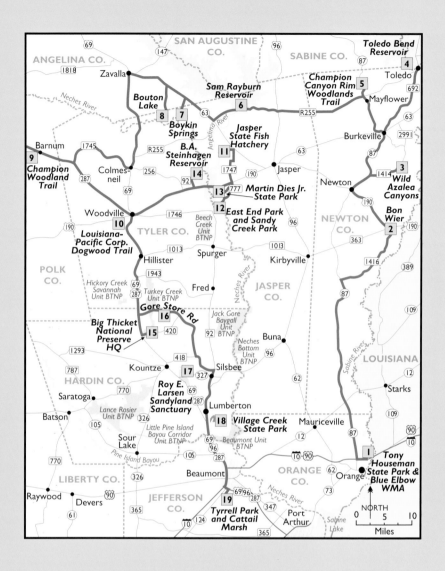

Toledo Bend
Reservoir

ANGELINA CO.

SAN AUGUSTINE
CO.

SABINE CO.

69

1818

147

96

87

4

Zavalla

Toledo

692

Bouton
Lake

8

7

Boykin
Springs

63

Sam Rayburn
Reservoir

6

Champion
Canyon Rim
Woodlands
Trail

5

Mayflower

R255

63

Jasper
State Fish
Hatchery

Burkeville

2991

Barnum

1745

R255

B.A.
Steinhagen
Reservoir

11

63

87

9

Champion
Woodland
Trail

287

Colmes-
neil

256

14

1747

190

Jasper

Newton

1414

3

Wild
Azalea
Canyons

69

92

13

777

Martin Dies Jr.
State Park

190

Bon
Wier

Woodville

10

1746

12

East End Park
and Sandy
Creek Park

96

NEWTON
CO.

2

190

190

Louisiana-
Pacific Corp.
Dogwood Trail

TYLER CO.

Beech
Creek
Unit
BTNP

363

Hillister

1013

Spurger

1013

Kirbyville

1416

389

1943

POLK
CO.

Hickory Creek
Savannah
Unit BTNP

69

287

Turkey Creek
Unit BTNP

Fred

JASPER
CO.

87

109

Gore Store Rd

16

Jack Gore
Baygall
Unit
BTNP

Big Thicket
National
Preserve
HQ

15

420

92

BTNP

Buna

96

Neches
Bottom
Unit
BTNP

LOUISIANA

1293

418

12

787

Kountze

17

327

Silsbee

62

Starks

HARDIN CO.

770

Roy E.
Larsen
Sandyland
Sanctuary

69

287

Lumberton

109

Saratoga

Lance Rosier
Unit BTNP

326

18

Village Creek
State Park

Mauriceville

87

90

Batson

105

Sour
Lake

Little Pine Island
Bayou Corridor
Unit BTNP

69

Beaumont Unit
BTNP

96

12

10

I

Tony
Houseman
State Park &
Blue Elbow
WMA

770

Pine Island Bayou

105

287

10

90

ORANGE
CO.

62

Orange

73

LIBERTY CO.

326

Beaumont

69 96

Neches River

NORTH

Raywood

Devers

90

JEFFERSON
CO.

365

19

Tyrrell Park
and Cattail
Marsh

287

347

Port
Arthur

Sabine
Lake

0   5   10

61

10

124

365

Miles

Big Thicket Loop

During April, Southeast Texas is a global focal point for spring migration. In summer it provides more than a million acres of habitat in which to observe and listen to a significant diversity of breeding birds. Pitcher plant sphagnum bogs, cypress swamps, and hardwood forests combine here to create a unique and beautiful mosaic for the visiting birder. North of Beaumont and west of the Sabine River, the longleaf pine forest, bald cypress stands, and riparian thickets host a rich assemblage of nesting birds. The damp morning air vibrates with a dawn chorus of at least fourteen species of warblers and is punctuated with the songs of flycatchers, vireos, tanagers, and buntings. Visitors will hear American Redstart, Louisiana Waterthrush, Black-and-white Warbler, Yellow-throated Warbler, Northern Parula, Hooded Warbler, Kentucky Warbler, Swainson's Warbler, Prairie Warbler, and Worm-eating Warbler amid the lush forest. Birds that passed silently through the coastal migrant traps just a few miles to the south—the first sheltering wooded patches they encountered after the long flight from the south—will now be bursting into song.

Planks sawn from longleaf pine over one hundred years ago can be found in the floors of stately old southern homes. The Texas Pineywoods retain a few old growth stands of this valuable tree. The fact that the longleaf pine forests depended on summer fires to ravage the underbrush and let the young pines grow meant that grass savannas grew beneath the trees. Standing in longleaf woods is unlike any other experience—surrounded by majestic trees, yet standing in a grassland.

The Red-cockaded Woodpecker makes its home exclusively in live old growth pines infected with red-heart disease. The bird has made a comeback as government agencies, private conservation groups, and members of the paper industry have combined to restore and preserve longleaf habitat. East Texas is one of the few places in North America to see this bird. The U.S. Forest Service has adopted summer burns, without which this great tree, and the wildlife that depends

FINDING WOODLAND BIRDS

Finding a variety of woodland birds involves visiting a variety of woodland habitats. Since all woodland birds are not uniformly distributed through all forests, discrimination between deciduous and nondeciduous, swampy and dry, pine and oak will increase exposure to a variety of species.

The problem with birding the Big Thicket versus birding Bolivar Flats is straightforward: the presence of two canopies and dim light obscures the line of sight. The forest may seem to be an endless layer of leaves. More than in any other habitat type, woodland birding depends on being guided by ear. Let every sound, every rustle, every click guide your eyes. Intrusive sounds such as woodpeckers banging on trees are sure cues that the alert birder will want to follow up. In woodlands, bird from sound to sound rather than from place to place.

Although double canopy birding presents a challenge, woodland birds do make significant amounts of noise in late spring and early summer, drawing attention to themselves for purposes of breeding and territorial defense. Any sound, even if down among the leaves, warrants a look. It could be a rabbit or a Wood Thrush, and the only way to find out is to listen, then look. Birds that are located while feeding on the ground are often less likely to pay attention to the observer and may provide a longer period of viewing.

Woodland birding in the Big Thicket, when done in spring and early summer, can be much easier than birding coastal woodlands during migration, because on the coast the birds are in transit and consequently silent. Once they arrive at the Big Thicket, they begin to vocalize. When singing on territory, birds such as the Hooded Warbler may sing from a perch for several minutes before going to the next branch. Thus in addition to cuing the birder to the bird's location, vocalization results in extended views of the bird.

Even after locating a sound, it is sometimes extremely difficult to pinpoint the bird. When birding with friends, one excellent tactic is to have everyone point to where they hear the bird and triangulate on the sound. For ventriloquial birds such as owls, point at the sound, move forward, point again, and repeat the process until the bird is in view.

Given the importance of careful listening in woodland habitat, it would seem obvious that talking should be kept to a minimum. Visitors who leave the pine thickets announcing that they "didn't see anything" may have been carrying on a lively conversation the entire time.

When all else fails, and with woodland birding this may happen repeatedly, it helps to recognize that birds were not put on earth for our entertainment. Roger Tory Peterson said that some birds will always elude positive identification, and as visitors to their habit, we simply have to derive satisfaction from the glance or the rustle or the song.

Water plays a major role in the Big Thicket. Birding by canoe and staking out river crossings increase the chance of locating woodland birds here. A number of target birds that people may miss at High Island may be singing on territory if looked for in the Thicket. Prothonotary, Yellow-throated, Swainson's, and Worm-eating warblers, Yellow-throated Vireo, and Painted Bunting all occur in these woodlands.

Kentucky Warbler

RAB/Naturewide Images

upon it, cannot survive. The Big Thicket Loop has several locations characterized by longleaf pine. The trail route allows visitors to drink in not only the beauty of the birds but the history and grandeur of the forests in which they once flourished.

Other recreational opportunities abound in East Texas. There are reservoirs renowned for bass fishing, and a plethora of bed-and-breakfast accommodations and campgrounds are nestled among birding habitats. Plant guides written especially for East Texas illustrate the amazing plant diversity here, including lilies, irises, three families of carnivorous plants, at least seventeen kinds of orchids, and an incredible variety of mushrooms. On top of all this, the

Big Thicket offers some of the finest canoeing in the state. Floating downriver in the company of Swallow-tailed Kites and beneath a forest canopy thick with wildlife is as good as it gets in the world of watchable wildlife. Butterflies and dragonflies also abound here; entomologist John Abbott has documented over one hundred dragonfly and damselfly species in the Big Thicket alone, more than one-fifth of the total for all of North America. Opportunities for nature photography are endless. No matter how much time visitors allot for this luxuriant habitat, most of it will remain unexplored, leaving ample reason to come back again and again.

RAB/Naturewide Images

Black-shouldered Spinyleg

Tony Houseman State Park and Blue Elbow Swamp Wildlife Management Area

RAB/Naturewide Images

1: Tony Houseman State Park and Blue Elbow Swamp Wildlife Management Area

Migrations, Summer
Free, Daily
Rating: 2
On I-10 entering Texas from Louisiana, just west of the Sabine River.

This site's boardwalk gives visitors an intimate view of the swamp, bottomland hardwoods, and mixed upland forest along the Sabine River. Tony Houseman State Park has Texas blueflag, trumpet creeper vine, red maple (unusual in Texas), sweetgum, and swamp chestnut. This site allows birders to view a type of habitat that is typically accessible only by boat and is well worth stopping to see. Note that the boardwalk must be accessed through the Texas Travel Information Center. Although the state park and wildlife management area extends west from this Center on both north and south sides of I-10, the boardwalk is the only public access point.

The park covers more than three thousand acres, with substantial wetland habitat. On even a short stroll down the boardwalk during spring or summer, Pileated Woodpecker can be seen here. Red-eyed Vireo, White-eyed Vireo, Acadian Flycatcher,

Northern Parula, Swainson's Warbler, Hooded Warbler, Prothonotary Warbler, and Yellow-throated Warbler all breed near the elevated boardwalk. Scan back across the Sabine River for a glimpse of the national bird—Bald Eagles nest on the Louisiana side. Yellow-throated Vireos nest here but are hard to spot because they prefer to sing cloaked among the leaves as they forage. Other wildlife includes white-tailed deer, feral hogs, raccoon, Virginia opossum, eastern gray squirrel, cottonmouth, eastern coral snake, western ribbon snake, and broad-banded water snake.

2: Bon Wier

Spring, Summer
Free, Daily
Rating: 1
From I-10, TX 87 N; FM 1416 E; FM 1416 N; US 190 E about 1.7 miles. At the birding trail sign, turn north onto a gravel road to the Sabine River. Parking is available by the bridge at the end of the drive.

Acadian Flycatcher and Yellow-throated Vireo are residents, but the primary draw of Bon Wier is the concentration of Swallow-tailed Kites that nest in the area from April until September. The kites are often seen above the woodlands bordering the Sabine River from this bridge, which is 2.2 miles from Bon Wier on US 190. Easy to identify, these black-and-white birds have long, pointed wings and deeply forked tails. Rarely flapping their wings, they continuously rotate their tails in flight. Locals may refer to these birds as "Scissor-tailed Hawks."

This mixed woodlands—mature hardwoods, along the river, and with substantial understory—is great for migrants. During spring migration the trees around the bridge can be filled with warblers and other birds, particularly if they are forced down after being caught by a sudden late spring cold front during their flight across the Gulf of Mexico.

Swallow-tailed Kite

Glenn Hayes/KAC Productions

TLE

White-tailed Kite

FINDING KITES

Three species of kites occur regularly on the Upper Texas Coast. At one time, Swallow-tailed Kite was the characteristic summer bird of the Houston area, but it declined and has become one of the rarest breeding birds in the state. Small but growing numbers now nest along the Sabine, Trinity, and Neches rivers, and a few are also seen in migration. Any open stretches of water along these rivers should be checked. Mississippi Kites nest in riparian forests, particularly pecan trees, in bottomlands along the Brazos River. Brazos Bend State Park, Cullinan Park, and Brazos River County Park (sites 117, 95, and 116) are all good sites to find these kites in spring and summer. Significant numbers migrate through the Upper Texas Coast in fall; look for them at the Smith Point Hawk Watch, in the pine woodlands of Memorial Park (site 93), and along the major bayous in Houston. The White-tailed Kite is a regular though uncommon breeder immediately along the coast, becoming increasingly common in winter. It is easily found at Galveston Island State Park. Later morning through midday is the best time for finding kites.

RAB/Naturewide Images

Hoary Azalea, Wild Azalea Canyons

3: Wild Azalea Canyons

Spring, Summer
Free, Daily
Rating: 2
From US 190; FM 2626 N; TX 87
N 1.0 mile; FM 1414 E 6.6 miles to
road marked Wild Azalea Canyons.
Turn right, follow signs for 2 miles to
Temple-Inland Wilderness Park.

The directions above guide you
through some of the back roads of
East Texas and are great for birding,
although shoulders for parking are
not always available. For the less
adventurous, or those with less time,
the site may be accessed via the town
of Newton (US 190 to TX 87), but
you would miss the great roads. The
roads pass through several stages of
regenerated pine forest that host such
species as Greater Roadrunner, Prairie Warbler, and Red-headed Woodpecker. Watch for Eastern Bluebirds
in the more open areas.

Northeast of Newton, off Texas
Highway 87, there are spectacular
canyons noted for longleaf pine
forests, two- to three-million-year-
old geological formations, and wild
azaleas that bloom in spring. Since
the 1880s, these canyons have provided naturalists with a beautiful and
surprising landform that contrasts
with the predominantly flat Texas
coast. Temple-Inland Forest Products
Corporation owns and maintains the
park. The azaleas begin blooming
in mid-March and continue through
early April. Steep paths can prove
treacherous due to the slick carpet
of pine needles, so walk with care.
Worm-eating, Hooded, and Swain-

son's warblers occur here, as do birds associated with pine habitat, such as Pileated Woodpecker, Wood Thrush, and Summer Tanager.

A numbered loop trail with several shortcuts descends into the shady canyon where the azaleas are found; the botanical spectacle should entice even avid birders. Along the Wild Azalea Canyon trail, listen for the buzz of Worm-eating Warbler, a relatively local breeder in East Texas. Take care not to disturb or remove any of the vegetation in this area.

Additional wildlife watching opportunities exist in and around Newton and may be of interest to people who pause for lodging or a meal.

Consider visiting Caney Creek Nature Park, one block east of Newton's courthouse square, and the Sylvan Nature Trail, which is four miles southeast of Newton on US 190, directly opposite the Texas Department of Transportation roadside park. Whispering Creek RV Park and Motel, 2.5 miles east of the Newton Courthouse on US 190, has a small nature trail that attracts a variety of woodland birds that changes with the seasons.

Before visiting Wild Azalea Canyons, note the following: The roads within the park may be confusing. The entrance road off FM 1414 is marked clearly, but there are very few signs within the park (and many

Worm-eating Warbler

FINDING WORM-EATING WARBLERS

This bird can be located by an atonal buzz that sounds more like a cricket or grasshopper than a bird. At Wild Azalea Canyons this bird is best seen in the early morning because it sings early and stops early—the performance is called the dawn chorus for a reason! The Worm-eating Warbler's song is easily missed because it resembles so many unbirdlike insect sounds. Pay particular attention to vine tangles as this is one of the few North American birds that habitually forages in dead curled leaves.

forks in the road to choose from) that direct you to the trailhead. You may notice two arrow signs directing you to the trailhead, which is a couple of miles from the entrance on FM 1414. The winding and hilly roads are soft, red dirt that becomes potholed and wet during the rains. Drive slowly and carefully. It may help to take a few notes on the way in to help retrace your way back to the entrance. Damage from Hurricane Rita closed the trail for awhile, but it is now open again to visitors.

4: Toledo Bend Reservoir, Sabine National Forest

All Seasons
Free, Daily
Rating: 1
TX 87 N; FM 692 N to
Toledo Bend Reservoir.

The Toledo Bend area marks the end point of El Camino Real, the road blazed in 1691 as a way to connect Monclova on the Rio Grande to the Spanish missions along the Sabine River. Toledo Bend Reservoir is sixty-five miles long, covers 190,000 surface acres of water, and spans the boundary between Texas and Louisiana.

Compared to other large lakes, Toledo Bend is underbirded, so time spent here could turn up unusual sightings. The observation site at the reservoir, located in Newton County, offers a look at breeding species of interest that include Broad-winged and Red-shouldered hawks as well as Osprey and Bald Eagle, both of which are uncommon in the region. Also occurring here are Chuck-will's-widow, Great Crested and Acadian flycatchers, Brown-headed Nuthatch, and Yellow-throated and Red-eyed vireos (and listen for the locally rare Warbling Vireo); Wood Thrush, American Redstart, and Louisiana Waterthrush; other warblers such as

Broad-winged Hawk

Black-and-white, Yellow-throated, Pine, Worm-eating, Swainson's, Kentucky, and Hooded; and Summer Tanager, Chipping and Bachman's sparrows, and Blue Grosbeak. Forest edge, scrubby areas, or stands of short pines produce species including Prairie Warbler, Yellow-breasted Chat, Indigo and Painted buntings, Eastern Towhee, and Lark Sparrow.

In addition, watch for birds passing along the river below the dam. The spillway offers an excellent vantage point from which to search for Swallow-tailed Kite, Bald Eagle, and other raptors drifting above the woods, for a variety of large waders, and in early morning for Wood Ducks departing their forest roosts. It is difficult to access the woodlands here—visitors can walk along the edge a little, but there are no trails.

During winter, check the large rafts of waterfowl for rarities.

5: Canyon Rim Woodlands Trail

Spring, Summer
Free, Daily
Rating: 2
TX 87 1.5 miles N of R (Recreational) 255 to trail.

Canyon Rim has forty-foot embankments lined with beech, southern magnolia, oak, and loblolly pine, the bluffs descending to clear-running springs and creeks in the bottom. The forest canopy provides instant relief from the noonday sun, and the canyon walls offer hikers some visible surface geology, which is rare on the Upper Texas Coast segments of the birding trail.

The canyon trail breaks off into three sections of easy, moderate, and difficult terrain. Trail signage does a good job of interpreting most of the canyon's significant vegetation as well as the interesting cankers and galls on the tree trunks that have resulted from insect or woodpecker damage. One sign marks a longleaf pine stump, demonstrating the scoring on the trunk that woodsmen once made with axes to collect pine pitch, another name for the tar the British bought for caulking the sailing ships in Britannia's fleet. Adorned with lichen-mottled bark, the beeches and other hardwoods that people normally do not associate with Texas—cherry, maple, and green ash—are stately and beautiful to behold.

Black-and-white Warblers, which prefer mixed pine and hardwood forests, nest along the trail. Identify this warbler by its squeaky, high-pitched song that resembles a creaky sewing machine. During spring and summer, many of the Big Thicket's characteristic woodland birds may be seen here. Near the Newton-Sabine county line Highway 87 bisects an active Red-cockaded Woodpecker nesting site.

Alan Murphy, www.AlanMurphyPhotography.com

Black-and-white Warbler

East Texas can be a challenging place to bird because of the dense cover, which often forces the observer to look through two canopies. Patience pays big dividends here. Excellent camouflage also adds to the challenge, and rather than striding purposefully along the trails, a slow pace interspersed with frequent stops will yield more and better views.

Louisiana Waterthrush nests along the creek flowing through the bottom of the canyon; during spring and summer listen for Blue-gray Gnatcatcher, Yellow-throated Vireo, and Red-eyed Vireo.

6: Sam Rayburn Reservoir and Angelina National Forest

All Seasons
Free, Daily
Rating: 1
TX 87 to R 255 W 8.0 miles to reservoir.

Sam Rayburn Reservoir, created by the impoundment of the Angelina River, covers close to 115,000 acres. Cypress and cherrybark oak have been planted around the edges of the reservoir. A control gate can flood up to thirteen acres for waterfowl habitat improvement. The reservoir is excellent for viewing waterfowl during fall migration and winter.

Rayburn Country, another excel-

lent area for Red-cockaded Woodpecker and Bachman's Sparrow, is a
subdivision en route to the reservoir.
Along the dirt roads just north of Eb-
enezer Park there are several active
Red-cockaded Woodpecker groups.
Many of the parks in the vicinity have
full-service camping facilities. Laughing and Ring-billed gulls, Black and
Caspian terns, and Neotropic Cormorant can all be seen here. This site is
also a good place to look for eastern
Wild Turkey.

Brown-headed Nuthatch

FINDING BROWN-HEADED NUTHATCHES

This relatively common bird can
be found in stands of restored
longleaf pine such as those on the
entrance road to Boykin Springs.
Brown-headed Nuthatches are
often heard well before they are
seen. Listen for a squeaky sound
high in the canopy. They congregate in groups and are easiest to
find in spring and summer when
the noisy young birds are out and
about. Watch for them among the
branches and pinecones, not along
the main trunks where other nuthatches feed.

Osprey

7: Boykin Springs Recreation Area, Angelina National Forest

Spring, Summer
Site fee, Daily
Rating: 2
R 255 W; TX 63 N 6.9 miles; FM 313
S 1.6 miles to the fork in the road.

Boykin Springs and the campground are closed indefinitely due to hurricane damage. However, Sexton Pond and a nearby Red-cockaded Woodpecker nesting area are still accessible.

From the fork in the road (FM 313 and FM 326), travel 1 mile on FM 326 past Sexton Pond on the left. At the one mile mark, notice that some of the tree trunks on the left side of the road are painted with rings. These are nesting trees of Red-cockaded Woodpeckers. They are best seen early in the morning, within the first half-hour of sunrise. Bachman's Sparrows and Brown-headed Nuthatches can be heard here as well. Birding the area by the pond, and a few side roads, it is possible to find Pine Warbler, Kentucky Warbler, and Wood Thrush. This is also a great place to find eastern Wild Turkey.

8: Upland Island Wilderness, Bouton Lake, and Sawmill Trail, Angelina National Forest

Spring, Summer
Site fee, Daily
Rating: 3
TX 63 to Roland Marshall Road/FM 303 and go S 7.8 miles to Bouton Lake. Note that much of Roland Marshall Road/FM 303 from TX 63 is a gravel dirt road with many potholes, so drive cautiously.

Natural lakes are rare in Texas—not counting the twenty thousand ephemeral rain-fed playa lakes in the Panhandle—and Bouton Lake would be a rare find even if the Lone Star State were as pockmarked with natural lakes as Minnesota. Stately bald cypress drapes the shoreline. Bouton (pronounced "Bowton") Lake and Boykin Springs are connected by an

RAB/Naturewide Images

Southern Sprite

Greg W. Lasley/KAC Productions

Bachman's Sparrow

FINDING BACHMAN'S SPARROWS

Look for this bird in bluestem grasslands that make up the understory of fire-maintained longleaf pine. If there is a scattering of yaupon in among the bluestem, you are in perfect habitat. These secretive and hard-to-see sparrows are most readily found in late spring and early summer, when the males are singing and several may be audible at once. At this time of year they are extraordinarily bold and can be located in low pine boughs. They are extremely difficult to see at other times of the year, and even if flushed will immediately flit to another clump of grass and secrete themselves. Although they may sing all day, try to arrive early (before traffic noises drown out their sweet minor trills), go into the longleaf pine, listen, then look.

old logging path, which is now inaccessible because of hurricane damage. The Aldridge Sawmill Trail is also closed. Bouton Lake campground has seven primitive campsites, no running water, and solitude by the bucketload.

Easily found summer woodland birds include Ruby-throated Hummingbird, Pileated, Downy, and Hairy woodpeckers (the latter now actually rare and local in this area), Acadian Flycatcher, White-eyed, Yellow-throated, and Red-eyed vireos, Northern Parula, Kentucky Warbler, Hooded Warbler, and Summer Tana-

RAB./Naturewide Images

Zebra Swallowtail

ger. The screams of Red-shouldered Hawks intensify the sensations of nature at the tranquil, pine-encircled lakeside. Louisiana Waterthrush and Swainson's Warbler nest along the tannin-stained streams that permeate the bottomland woods.

Bouton Lake and all the neighboring Pineywoods locations offer the naturalist a variety of large, showy swallowtail butterflies, including Eastern Tiger, Spicebush, Palamedes, Pipevine, and Zebra swallowtails. All are relatively common around their preferred food plants. Even the casual observer will notice these beautiful creatures as they flit along the sunny roadsides. The area is also considered to be among the richest in the state for orchids.

9: Long-Leaf Pine Woodland Trail

Spring, Summer
Free, Daily
Rating: 1
US 69 to FM 1745 W 13.7 miles; US 287 N 6.0 miles; FM 62 S 0.4 mile. Trail on left.

The main appeal of this site is its tremendous longleaf pine forest, one of the few remaining old growth stands left in Texas. The mixture of old and young trees gradually blends into a

FINDING HENSLOW'S SPARROWS

© Jim Morgan

Henslow's Sparrow

This bird was known through the 1970s as a breeder near Hobby Airport in Houston but is now extirpated there. The only individuals on the Upper Texas Coast are wintering birds. Look for moist stands of bluestem under longleaf pine forests in East Texas: Boykin Springs and Bouton Lake are prime habitat for this decidedly ground-loving species. Henslow's Sparrow is not usually inclined to respond to *pisshing,* so walking into the habitat is often required.

hardwood forest that provides excellent habitat for typical woodland species. A Red-cockaded Woodpecker group borders the site, and American Kestrels have nested here.

10: Louisiana-Pacific Corporation Dogwood Trail

Spring, Summer
Free, Daily
Rating: 2
US 287 to US 69 S in Woodville for 0.4 mile; US 190 E 3.0 miles to LPC Dogwood Trail on left.

Dogwood, of which there are about fifty varieties globally and about seventeen in the United States, was ideal for the manufacture of arrows. In both the New World and the Old it is known by such names as arrow-wood and Indian arrow-wood. The Dogwood Trail, conveniently accessed from the town of Woodville, is another site to check for eastern woodland species. Pine Warblers trill in the canopy throughout much of the year and are joined in spring by Black-and-white and Hooded warblers, Northern Parula, Red-eyed and Yellow-throated vireos, and Indigo Bunting. During winter, listen for feeding flocks within the trees, and then call them in for closer viewing by making *pisshing* sounds. Your first response may be the plaintive note of a

Blue-gray Gnatcatcher, to be followed by the *seet* of an Orange-crowned Warbler or the rapid ticking of a Ruby-crowned Kinglet. Blue-headed Vireo, Yellow-bellied Sapsucker, and several locally nesting woodpeckers often attend these winter aggregations. Pileated Woodpeckers nest here and are easiest to see (and hear) during spring.

Butterflies such as Zebra, Palamedes, and Spicebush swallowtails are often common here. After late March, watch sunny spots on the trail or along the margin of the parking area for Southern Pearly Eye, a large brown butterfly of the southeastern forests. Note the arc of prominent eyespots on the underside of the hind wing, all surrounded by a broad white border. This species is considerably larger and more locally distributed than the Gemmed and Carolina satyrs and Little Wood Satyr that also fly here. The Dogwood Trail is particularly beautiful in early April, when

Blooming dogwood

Snowy Egret

a local festival celebrates the brief appearance of this lovely tree's creamy white blossoms.

11: Jasper State Fish Hatchery

All Seasons
Free, Daily
Rating: 1
US 190 to FM 1747 N 4.2 miles; FM 2799 E for 0.8 mile; FM 1747 N for

1.6 mile; County Road 009 W 0.6 mile to Jasper State Fish Hatchery.

The hatchery ponds are laid out on a grid and surrounded by mowed grassy dikes. The ponds contain largemouth bass, channel catfish, hybrid sunfish, smaller forage species, and a few ornamental carp. Pineywoods surround the perimeter of the hatchery, offering excellent edge birding without the traffic associated with roadsides. The ponds attract grebes, a few migrating ducks, Anhinga, cormorants, Bald Eagle, Osprey, longer-legged shorebirds, and a variety of large wading birds. Reptiles and amphibians also make use of these aquatic habitats. The area is excellent for dragonflies and good for butterflies; during late March and early April six species of swallowtails occur on the property. Most can be found nectaring on hoary azaleas growing at the south side of the pond complex. The forest bordering the hatchery can be good for woodland birds, including several species of warblers and vireos.

The hatchery is open Monday to Friday from 8:00 A.M. to 5:00 P.M. Weekend visits or those earlier or later during the week can be confirmed by calling the hatchery staff at (409) 384-2221.

RAB/Naturewide Images

American Alligator

12: East B. A. Steinhagen Reservoir

All Seasons
Free, Daily
Rating: 1
US 190 to FM 777 S 1.2 mile; County Road 155 N 2.2 miles to U.S. Army Corps of Engineers Sandy Creek Park. After visiting this area, take FM 777 S 2.9 miles to the Corps' East End Park/Town Bluff Project.

This site's mixed hardwood bottomland forest is home to nesting species such as Yellow-throated Vireo and Kentucky, Prothonotary, Hooded, and Swainson's warblers. Typically these birds are already here singing on territory in late March and early April when most birders are searching for them in the coastal migrant traps. Naturally, these woods attract numbers of spring and fall migrants, especially during rain or cold fronts, but they are difficult to see because their numbers are not as concentrated as when in the coastal oak and hackberry mottes. During summer most of the Pineywoods breeding birds are present: listen for Pileated Woodpeckers excavating in dead timber, the Summer Tanager's coarse robinlike delivery, and the Red-eyed Vireo's endless and rather monotonous delivery of short, chopped phrases. The

reservoir itself is excellent for seeing alligators. These attractive and
enigmatic reptiles are more difficult
to see outside their coastal habitat,
and Steinhagen's environs provide a
number of good viewing opportunities. Waterbird or dragonfly photographers working the water's edge
should devote one eye to alligator
watching, lest they end up treading
on a twelve-foot reptile. Watch also
for the Bald Eagles that occasionally
nest in this vicinity; they are more
numerous during winter. Eagles may
be seen during the locally available
guided canoe trips that put in on the
Angelina River and float down to the
reservoir, providing superb viewing
opportunities for Swallow-tailed Kites
and the area's many nesting waders.
For canoe trip information, inquire at
Martin Dies Jr. State Park.

13: Martin Dies Jr. State Park

All Seasons
Site fee, Daily
Rating: 2
US 190 to Park Road 48 S 2.9 miles
to park headquarters and get park
map. The Hen House Ridge Unit is
south of US 190.

Martin Dies consists of three separate
units: Cherokee, Walnut Ridge, and
Hen House Ridge. Both the Cherokee
and Walnut Ridge units are closed

indefinitely due to hurricane damage, but the Hen House Ridge unit
remains open.

The parkland, located on the
western edge of the Big Thicket, is
generally flat and contains a mixture
of pine and riverbottom hardwoods.
Beech, magnolia, sweet bay, cypress,
and willow trees make a picturesque
backdrop along shallow sloughs. During the fall, golden beeches and reddish hues of black gum and oak trees
strike up stunning contrasts with the
evergreen pine needles.

Pileated Woodpecker

The bottomland forests of the South once covered 24 million acres of land throughout the floodplain of the Lower Mississippi River Valley, stretching from southern Illinois to coastal Louisiana. Bottomland forest habitat is a crucial niche for numerous animals and plants; roughly 80 percent of our breeding birds require it for survival. North America's rarest songbird, Bachman's Warbler, if it is not extinct, may still survive in the remaining bottomland forest areas of the Lower Mississippi Valley. Bottomland habitat, including that of the lower Neches River, provides spawning, nursery, and feeding habitat for warm-water fish. It enhances water quality by removing excess nutrients and pollutants and reduces erosion by providing settling areas for particles suspended in the water column. Additionally, revenues from fishing, canoeing, birdwatching, and hunting contribute significantly to the region's economy.

The Neches River, which flows out of Steinhagen Reservoir, provides some of the best canoeing in the country, and a put-in just downstream of the park provides visitor access to the heart of the Big Thicket. The Angelina-Neches Scientific Area and Dam B Wildlife Management Area, situated north of the park, are accessible only by boat.

Listen for the locally common Pileated Woodpecker all year, and Brown Creeper in winter. During winter, this area remains productive; the remaining wading birds and resident woodland species are joined by loons, grebes, ducks and geese, gulls, a few shorebirds including American Woodcock, Bald Eagle, other raptors, and large flocks of wintering icterids. Watch especially for Rusty Blackbird where the wooded understory is flooded or damp.

14: West B. A. Steinhagen Reservoir

All Seasons
Site fee, Daily
Rating: 2
The Walnut Ridge and Cherokee units of Martin Dies Jr. State Park are along the western edge of the reservoir, accessed from US 190. Obtain maps at park headquarters.

Eastern Kingbird

Although the Walnut Ridge and Cherokee units of Martin Dies Jr. State Park are closed indefinitely due to hurricane damage, parking and access to Steinhagen Reservoir is still available.

In the winter this is one of the better places to see ducks. Unusual sightings include Cinnamon Teal, and this part of the reservoir is also good for alligators. Along the western side of Steinhagen, just downstream from the bridge, is a heron rookery. In May, Martin Dies Jr. State Park offers a boat tour that goes up the river and terminates at the rookery. Cattle, Great, and Snowy egrets and Great Blue Heron all occur here. Nesting Eastern Kingbirds put on quite a display for onlookers as well. During winter this area remains productive.

To U.S. Army Corps of Engineers Magnolia Ridge Park: Less than a mile west of the reservoir, take FM 92 N 1.9 miles to the park.

To the Corps' Camper's Cove Park: FM 92 S to County Road 4130, 2.5 miles after crossing US 190; CR 4130 E 0.6 mile to the park.

15: Big Thicket National Preserve

All Seasons
Site fee, Daily
Rating: 3
Preserve headquarters and visitor center: US 69/287 at FM 420. Obtain detailed directions to the preserve's various units.

The Big Thicket National Preserve is not a contiguous stretch of habitat but rather a series of disjunct venues reflecting the conflicted legislative compromises that led to its creation. Despite its fractured character, it is the premier wildlife watching area in East Texas. A visitor center provides information about the preserve's various units and should be consulted before selecting your route. The Kirby Nature Trail, a short drive from the center, offers wheelchair access and is a good venue for woodpeckers, Hooded Warbler, Yellow-throated Vireo, Red-eyed Vireo, and other forest species. In spring, Pileated Woodpeckers are easily found here, and resident Barred Owls can be hooted up with a bit of effort. Carolina Chickadee, Tufted Titmouse, Downy Woodpecker, and Yellow-bellied Sapsucker can all be found here.

Much of the area along the Kirby Nature Trail looks wild and in its natural state, and the rich fragrance of the woods here is entrancing. The occasional appearance of a brilliantly colored Hooded Warbler and the ceaseless pulse of insect life in the forest is an incomparably fine experience. One stretch of the Kirby Nature Trail runs along a swamp bottom where a few tremendous old cypress trees remain, their mysterious knees poking up through the water. This region of East Texas is one of the most botanically diverse in North America. Desert cactus lives side by side with reindeer moss found commonly on the arctic tundra.

The Sundew Trail is one of the best birding areas within the preserve. Look for the tiny red, flat leaf rosettes of annual sundew, one of the Thicket's carnivorous plants. Sundews live on nutrient-poor soils and supplement their diet with living insects. Note that each leaf is covered with hairs, which secrete a sticky insect-digesting enzyme. Because the leaves do not close around the prey, the legs of a hapless bug may be left hanging on a leaf after the body has been ingested.

The Big Thicket also boasts superb canoeing below the dam at Steinhagen Reservoir. A forty-mile paddle provides solitude and exposure to much of the Thicket's rich birdlife.

RAB/Naturewide Images

Annual Sundew

16: Gore Store Road and Turkey Creek

Migrations, Summer
Site fee, Daily
Rating: 1
US 69/287 to Gore Store Road E 11.7 miles; Firetower Road S 0.1 mile; Camp Waluta Road S 1.8 miles; U-turn on Camp Waluta Road 1.8 mi; Firetower Road S 5.2 miles; Old Kountze Road S to FM 418. The roads themselves are birding sites.

Gore Store Road and the mature pine forests surrounding it were once renowned for birding, and birders came here from all over the world to find Pineywoods specialties such as the Red-cockaded Woodpecker, Brown-headed Nuthatch, Pine Warbler, and Bachman's Sparrow. Extensive timbering in the area has left these pine

Prairie Warbler

ting, and Painted Bunting. There are several good places along the road to listen for Prairie Warblers—just watch for plantations of small pine trees. Keep an eye open for soaring Broad-winged Hawks and Mississippi Kites. From late spring through early summer, listen for the Eastern Screech-Owl, Barred Owl, and Chuckwill's-widow just after dark or immediately before sunrise.

forests in a perpetual state of early succession, resulting in local extirpation of these species. Toledo Bend Reservoir and Boykin Springs are now more reliable sites for these specialties and constitute much more attractive habitat in which to seek them. However, species that prefer early succession growth and dense yaupon holly thickets, such as Prairie and Swainson's warblers, Yellow-breasted Chat, and Indigo and Painted buntings, are now fairly easy to find here. Red-headed Woodpeckers often nest in the dead trees. Listen for the Prairie Warbler's rising *zee, zee, zee, zee, zee* in young pine plantations and the ringing call of Swainson's Warbler wherever a bridge crosses a wooded creek bottom. Typically, the similar song of ten or twenty Hooded Warblers is heard for each Swainson's.

Firetower Road is often worth a look; the Eastern Towhee nests here, as do the Greater Roadrunner, Prairie Warbler, Blue Grosbeak, Indigo Bun-

This and other sandy roads in the Thicket can be treacherous after rain. Drive on the crown of the road and park on the flattest possible spots.

The Turkey Creek Trail, a walk that spans fifteen miles along the central part of the Big Thicket preserve, is on the north side a couple of miles down Gore Store Road. Portions of the trail are still pristine; taking a few minutes or hours to hike this trail will afford some of the most rewarding moments in East Texas.

17: Roy E. Larsen Sandyland Sanctuary

Spring, Summer
Free, Daily
Rating: 2
From US 69/287 FM 327 E;
sanctuary on right.

This site has some of the best stands of longleaf pine in the Big Thicket. The sanctuary is open year-round

FINDING PRAIRIE WARBLERS

This bird's preferred habitat is young pine plantations. As with Bachman's Sparrow, the key to finding the bird is locating the right habitat. The short, dense pine thickets that arise after a burn or in young pine plantations are prime Prairie Warbler habitat. Gore Store Road, and the countless pine plantations along the back roads, are good places to look for this bird. It is much more common during fall than spring migration. At coastal sites, look for it in habitat that is structurally similar to the short pines of East Texas; stands of salt cedar (tamarisk) are the likeliest place to find this bird during spring migration. Its voice is a distinctive high, buzzy sound that rises in pitch. Do not trespass on private land or pine plantations in search of this bird. It can typically be seen from the roadside.

Also, especially along Gore Store Road, look for oddly configured silhouettes on telephone wires or cables—Prairie Warblers are often seen singing from these perches.

except during dry summers, when fire danger is high. The self-guided trail, with maps and pamphlets at the trailhead, passes through dense and open woodlands and offers excellent opportunities to see or hear a representative selection of eastern woodland birds. Watch for the Barred Owl, which is often vocal; for woodpeckers, Acadian Flycatcher, and Brown-headed Nuthatch; and for Pine, Black-and-white, Prothonotary, Yellow-throated, and Hooded warblers, and Summer Tanager.

The river trail along Village Creek is one of the most scenic walks in the Thicket and also includes the most popular canoeing route in Texas. The lower three-mile floodplain trail is quiet and picturesque.

The arid pine sandhills plant association present at Roy E. Larsen is rare in the Big Thicket. Coarse quartz sands found at the surface trap neither nutrients nor the area's abundant rains. This desertlike habitat hosts such sand-loving species as sand jack (oak), Louisiana yucca, eastern prickly pear, weakstem sunflower, and Carolina vervain. Sunny days produce a variety of dragonflies and butterflies. During spring, watch for the locally uncommon Gray Petaltail, a large dragonfly considered by many to be a living fossil. Common odonates occurring along Village Creek include Black-shouldered

RAB/Naturewide Images

Gray Petaltail

Spinyleg, Slaty and Great Blue skimmers, and Ebony Jewelwing.

The juxtaposition of different habitats is among the traits of the Big Thicket area that make it such a superb place for nature viewing and such a natural candidate for permanent protection by the national government. Since animal and plant life depend upon vegetation, which in turn depends upon soil type, it is apt that this ecologically diverse region is thought to contain more than a hundred different soil types—more than anywhere else on earth. Hence the discovery in the Thicket of gourd vine (a plant native to the dry limestone creeks of Central Texas), ten species of West Texas wildflowers, one flower otherwise found only on the prairie,

and other plants that are native to southwestern deserts. The presence of an arid sandhill community in the traditional Big Thicket region, of which the Roy E. Larsen Sandyland Sanctuary is a part, reinforces the richness and natural beauty of the area.

18: Village Creek State Park

Migrations, Summer
Site fee, Daily
Rating: 2
Signage to park is just east of the junction of US 96 and US 69/287 in Lumberton.

This park has pristine white sand beaches that line the creek, the

FINDING SWAINSON'S WARBLERS

Swainson's Warbler is a special search item for most birders because it is geographically restricted to the southeastern United States. In Texas, Swainson's Warbler inhabits the understory of moist forest, often among palmetto, which serves as an indicator plant for this bird. Find it by paying attention to the vegetation, watching especially for deep woodland thickets with clumps of yaupon or palmetto palm. As if in concession to its choice of drab-colored habitat, the bird itself is one of our least colorful warblers. The compensation for its dull coloring is a loud voice that cuts through the woods. Listen for its loud and distinctive call: *Oo-oo-stepped-in-poo,* and you will have your bird.

Also look for this bird at Bear Creek Park, Boykin Springs, Tyrrell Park, and Sabine Woods (sites 97, 7, 19, and 26), to name only a few locations. The best viewing times are late spring and early summer.

Alan Murphy, www.AlanMurphyPhotography.com

Swainson's Warbler

RAB/Naturewide Images

Broad-headed Skink

remains of a bay that once went all the way up to Huntsville and Livingston.

The park has hiking access to Big Thicket habitats such as bald cypress-tupelo swamp and baygall areas. Floating down Village Creek to the park reveals the Thicket in all its beauty. Note, however, that Village Creek State Park does not have a canoe put-in, and the next takeout point downstream is in the middle of the Beaumont petrochemical complex. There is a tupelo trail in the park and a baygall habitat along the Caney Slough Trail. Most of the swampland had been logged by the beginning of the twentieth century, to the detriment of such species as the Ivory-billed Woodpecker and the previously abundant Wood Duck.

Baygall is a term used for a wet plant association underlain by impermeable clays. A baygall usually contains sweet bay, gallberry holly, and sphagnum moss. Many of the state's rarest flowers, including a variety of orchids, occur in this wet, acid environment, characterized by pitch-black water as jet as any barrel of West Texas crude. During late fall and early winter, watch for the towering white spikes of the orchid called fragrant ladies' tresses along the drying margins of cypress swamps. Geyata Ajilvsgi's *Wild Flowers of the Big Thicket, East Texas, and Western Louisiana* (1979) gives an interesting overview of this and other Big Thicket plant associations.

The relatively young mixed pine and hardwood forests host a repre-

sentative selection of eastern woodland birds; so far, over one hundred
species have been recorded here.
Short and long trails provide access
to the park's sloughs, lakes, and
rivers.

Organized birding tours are of-
fered at the park on a monthly basis.
Dragonflies and damselflies are plentiful in the various aquatic habitats,
and such butterflies as Palamedes and
Zebra swallowtails cruise the sunny
road margins.

19: Tyrrell Park and Cattail Marsh

All Seasons
Free, Daily
Rating: 2
US 96 to I-10 W in Beaumont;
Walden Road left, which becomes
Tyrrell Park Road; park on left.

Tyrrell Park is a multiuse facility that
retains sufficient habitat to support
an interesting selection of eastern
breeding birds as well as excellent
eighteen-hole habitat for the American golfer. During spring and summer
listen for Eastern Wood-Pewee, Acadian Flycatcher (uncommon), Great
Crested Flycatcher, Pine Warbler,
Swainson's Warbler (also uncommon), Hooded Warbler, and Summer
Tanager. Yellow-crowned Night-Herons stalk the golf course for crawfish.
The mud chimneys these crustaceans

Yellow-crowned Night-Heron

RAB/Naturewide Images

construct appear all over the boggy
upper coast. The park is an excellent
spot for seeing Fish Crows, especially
near the picnic tables, washrooms,
and shelters at the farthest end of the
loop road. In Texas this resident of the
easternmost edge of the upper coast
is rarely seen away from the Red/
Neches/Sabine River drainages. It is
easiest to identify by its call, which
resembles a high pitched *ennnnk*. The
American Crow outside of this region
has a number of calls that sound like
the Fish Crow. The best place to find
Fish Crows is Tyrrell Park, although
they are also easily seen in other Big
Thicket communities.

Least Grebe

Also look for Downy, Red-bellied, Red-headed, and Pileated woodpeckers, Eastern Kingbird, Great Crested Flycatcher, and the usual chickadee-titmouse flock, which may contain other birds, depending on the season. During a fallout the trees will be alive with migrants.

Cattail Marsh is part of Beaumont's wastewater treatment facility. This nine-hundred-acre artificial wetland attracts an incredible diversity of waterbirds throughout the year. The Beaumont area produces about 25 million gallons of wastewater per day.

After moving through seven hundred miles of pipes and being treated at the wastewater facility, the water is dumped into the marsh, where the plants and wildlife polish the water to a level of sanitation that is fit for reuse. The assortment of birds present on the ponds at any one time changes with the water level, so be prepared to scope as many ponds as possible. The shifting nature of bird concentrations as different species choose different sites makes Cattail Marsh an exciting and rewarding place to bird. In recent years the ponds have produced rarities such as Least Grebe and Long-tailed Duck. Taking more than a quick look during lunch or embarking on an extended crow hunt will require water, a spotting scope, and a comfortable pair of hiking shoes. Visitors may walk the various dikes; those that are not surfaced may be thickly covered with vegetation. During most months, the dikes are alive with dragonflies and butterflies.

The view of Cattail Marsh from atop the levee road, indeed the view upon entering Tyrrell Park itself, comes as a shock to the eye after the previous eighteen sites on the Big Thicket Loop. Oak trees draped with moss, the flat landscape, and the intense green of the permanently damp coastal plain provide a striking contrast to the dense cover of the Pineywoods.

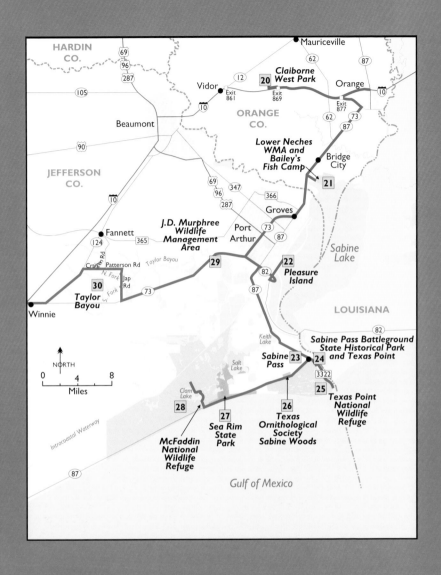

HARDIN CO.

69
96
287

105

Mauriceville

Vidor

12
20 Claiborne West Park

Exit 861
Exit 869

10

Orange

87

10

Exit 877

62
73

87

ORANGE CO.

62

Beaumont

90

JEFFERSON CO.

Lower Neches WMA and Bailey's Fish Camp

Bridge City

10

69
96
347
287

366

21

J.D. Murphree Wildlife Management Area

Groves

73

87

Fannett

124
365

Port Arthur

Sabine Lake

Patterson Rd

Taylor Bayou

29

82

22 Pleasure Island

Craigen Rd

N. Fork

S. Fork

Jap Rd

87

30 Taylor Bayou

73

LOUISIANA

Winnie

Keith Lake

82

NORTH

Salt Lake

Sabine Pass

23 24 Sabine Pass Battleground State Historical Park and Texas Point

0   4   8

Miles

Clam Lake

3322

25 Texas Point National Wildlife Refuge

28

27 Sea Rim State Park

26 Texas Ornithological Society Sabine Woods

Intracoastal Waterway

McFaddin National Wildlife Refuge

87

Gulf of Mexico

Sabine Loop

The most dramatic contrasts between consecutive sites on the Great Texas Coastal Birding Trail, and between the birding sites and their surroundings, are along the Sabine Loop. For example, the trail goes from a classic coastal marsh south of Beaumont to a mixed hardwood forest toward nearby Orange. The shifts impart a sense of the way nature weaves its ecosystems, sometimes with sharp breaks, sometimes in gradual shifts, and sometimes in vacillating switches from one kind of habitat to another and back again. In the Texas extension of the Sabine's wetland habitat lies one of the stranger couplings on the planet. On the one hand, the Beaumont–Port Arthur–Greater Houston area hosts the largest concentration of petrochemical manufacturing and refineries in the world. On the other, this area has some of the greatest avian diversity and finest birding venues in North America.

This part of the Upper Texas Coast is world renowned for its importance as a springtime landing zone for neotropical migrants, and several of the sites on this loop are "must visits" for travelers who have come in search of a spring migratory bonanza. The stretch of coast down to McFaddin National Wildlife Refuge is deserted for most of the year, providing a remote and appealing destination for the naturalist who prefers solitude. Conservation has played a critical role on this part of the trail, with landmark sites such as the Texas Ornithological Society's Sabine Woods being the tangible results of committed efforts to preserve critical habitat for migrating birdlife.

Fall migration on the Texas coast, although less publicized than the climaxes of spring, in many ways offers more significant opportunities for birding enthusiasts. Southbound migrants begin arriving in early July, with shorebirds such as the Semipalmated Plover, Greater and Lesser yellowlegs, and Western, Least, Solitary, Pectoral, and Upland sandpipers reaching the coast not long after spring migration ends in early June. The only months of the year when a sizable migration is not under way are June, January, and February,

Semipalmated Plover

continue to be good viewing seasons, particularly for birds that winter in northern Mexico, such as Black-throated Green Warbler and Black-and-white Warbler.

The drawback to birding the coast much past spring is the weather. The Texas coast can be scorchingly hot, and since the heat is combined with high humidity and especially prolific mosquitoes, fall birders should be prepared for adverse conditions. One might call this the time of year for "Gatorade birding": it begins not with October cold fronts but in the second week of July. Labor Day marks the peak of *Empidonax* flycatcher and gnatcatcher migration. The weather is swelteringly hot, but birders had best not wait until it gets cool later in the fall to bird for these migrants, because many will be long gone. Ana-huac National Wildlife Refuge, Sabine Woods, Sea Rim State Park, and High Island are all good fall sites. Sea Rim's Gambusia Trail is a super spot for Ga-torade birding, as is Brazoria National Wildlife Refuge.

which accounts for the exciting year-round nature of birding in this part of the state.

By the second week of July, Piping Plovers have returned to the coast, and by the end of July fall migration has begun in earnest, essentially continuing through December. Major waves are timed with the cold fronts sweeping out of Canada later in the fall. Groups such as the *Empidonax* flycatchers and Olive-sided Flycatcher are best seen later in the year because of their elliptical migration route, which takes them through Texas in significant numbers only in the fall. Neotropical migrants such as Nash-ville Warbler, Canada Warbler, and Warbling Vireo are also more easily seen in fall. Late fall and early winter

20: Claiborne West Park

All Seasons
Free, Daily
Rating: 1
I-10 W from TX 87 for 8.4 miles; exit freeway at exit 869, continue 2.4 miles on feeder road; park is on right.

Few places blend the woodland habitat of the Pineywoods and the marsh ecology of the coast with the elegance of this small park. At the entrance, a small trail leads off behind the information shed and goes through a remarkable stand of mixed hardwoods. Along the path stands a small but delightful specimen of black cherry, with surrounding white oak and loblolly pine. Claiborne West Park offers an impressive interpretive display for such a small facility. It is an excellent place to advance one's tree identification because many of the trees are labeled. For a few hundred yards of shaded path the tall, smooth-barked red cedar, a plethora of red oak and white oak, towering American elm, hickory, black willow, and loblolly pine look over the rest of the canopy, and beneath them are several nice samples of yaupon holly, an important food plant for wintering fruit-eaters.

Some of the resident turtles in the marsh have grown enormous, and a good selection of waterbirds occurs at the pond. The path continues up along a dike back into the park, where more birding opportunities await. Assorted Big Thicket woodland birds also come through Claiborne Park. Yellow-throated, Pine, and Prothonotary warblers nest in and around this park, and the Brown-headed Nuthatch (a locally diminishing species) is frequently seen in the area. During spring, and especially after a late season norther has blown in, the trees are full of migrants that have settled in the woods for a breather and a bite to eat.

21: Lower Neches Wildlife Management Area and Bailey's Fish Camp, Neches River

All Seasons
Free, Daily
Rating: 2
TX 73/87 S from Orange; Lake Street S 1.5 miles to Lower Neches WMA observation platform and Rob Bailey's Fish Camp.

The observation platform is down the road and overlooks a broad expanse of coastal marsh. Likely marsh

Little Blue Heron

RAB/Naturewide Images

birds include Clapper Rail, White and White-faced ibis, and Osprey. Continue south from the observation platform along the shell road, which leads to Rob Bailey's Fish Camp and Sabine Lake. Herons, egrets, spoonbills, waterfowl, and shorebirds mass in this area, so bring a spotting scope. In the past, this wildlife management area has been the site of a Swallow-tailed Kite watch.

Sabine Lake is formed by the mouths of the Sabine and Neches rivers, and while Louisiana can lay claim to at least half the Sabine, the Neches belongs to Texas alone. The Angelina and Neches River basins represent two of the most prolific river basins in the state. These two rivers tie together seventeen Texas counties encompassing approximately ten thousand square miles, and they dump close to one and a half billion gallons of water each year into the Gulf of Mexico.

22: Pleasure Island

All Seasons
Free, Daily
Rating: 1
TX 73/87 S to Groves. Remain on TX 73 S when the two roads divide in Groves; take TX 82 S 2.4 miles, cross Gulf Intracoastal Waterway on the MLK Bridge. Exit for the T. B. Ellison Parkway and Pleasure Island.

Loons, grebes, and waterfowl abound in the winter, so explore. The north and south ends of Pleasure Island can be loaded with birds; wander the levee roads and scope out the concentrations of ducks, gulls, and terns. When the south impoundment's muddy bottom is exposed, shorebirding can be very rewarding. The extraordinary variety of migrants can include White-rumped Sandpiper, Hudsonian Godwit, Pectoral Sandpiper, and American Golden-Plover.

The deeper water of Pleasure Island attracts more diving ducks than the Lower Neches WMA. Coastal marsh is a subtle habitat and not dramatic except for the huge flocks of ducks, geese, and pelicans that occur here. Its subtlety is one of the great beauties of the coastal marsh, and it requires that the visitor be attuned to the smallest of details in order to ferret out the wealth of attractions. Birding coastal marsh is an effort, except for the herons, egrets, gulls, and terns, which can be viewed with relative ease. Yet subtlety should not be understood to mean lack of importance: the coastal marsh fuels the entire bay ecosystem and is the primary source of detritus that feeds the various polychaetes and other worms, clams, shrimp, larval fishes, and other food sources for the bird species that occur here. This type of marsh along the Upper Texas Coast rates as one of the most productive habitats in the world.

TLE

White Ibis

Much of what is going on here is hidden. The marshes are filled with breeding rails. Clapper Rails call in the early morning and evening, but despite large populations they tend to be very secretive. Other rails enter the marsh habitat in winter, some of them among North America's most sought-after birds: the Black Rail, which breeds in small numbers in isolated colonies along the Texas coast but which is seldom seen, occurs here. Painstaking, well-timed, quiet, and deliberate efforts (or just dumb luck) are required to get good views of this bird.

The Yellow Rail is another bird to look for here and is common in rice fields and in the Anahuac National Wildlife Refuge. It arrives in fall, stays through winter, and then returns to Canada and Minnesota to breed; but as with Black Rail, it takes careful planning to see Yellow Rails

RAB/Naturewide Images

White-rumped Sandpiper

(see "Finding Rails" on page 105). Seaside Sparrow and Nelson's Sharp-tailed Sparrow are other attractive marsh birds, exciting to see but usually well hidden in the marsh until *pisshing* noises bring them into view.

23: Sabine Pass

All Seasons
Free, Daily
Rating: 1
TX 87 S to Sabine Pass marsh.

En route to the pass, Sabine Lake is on the left and Keith Lake on the right. Watch the lakes for Neotropic Cormorant, mostly in summer, as well as for waterfowl, gulls, and terns. Throughout the year the Sabine Pass marshes are an excellent place to scope for a variety of wetland species, including Least Bittern (summer), White Ibis, White-faced Ibis, Glossy Ibis (rare but possibly a local nester), Roseate Spoonbill, Little Blue Heron, Tricolored Heron, Clapper Rail, Common Yellowthroat, and Seaside Sparrow. Listen for this sparrow's song, a miniature, high-pitched rendition of that of the Red-winged Blackbird. The nesting grackle in this marsh is the Boat-tailed, and a small percentage of Boat-tailed Grackles in this area have yellow eyes, as they do

RAB/Naturewide Images

Tricolored Heron

24: Sabine Pass Battleground State Historical Park (now State Park and Historic Site) and Texas Point

All Seasons, particularly Spring
Free, Daily
Rating: 1
From Sabine Pass, FM 3322 S to Sabine Pass Battleground State Park. Continue on FM 3322 E; right on South 1st 3.5 miles to dead-end at Pilot Station and Texas Point.

The trees and shrubs at this site attract a variety of migrants in spring and fall. Upon entering the park, note that besides marsh grass, the acreage

in the eastern United States. Half a mile south of the marsh is the small community of Sabine Pass, which was inundated by the floodwaters of Hurricane Rita and is now rebuilding. Here visitors can get snacks and mosquito repellent.

In the town, a historical marker identifies the old Sabine Pass cemetery. The large oak trees here provide shelter for spring migrants that have just made landfall after flying through a cold front; the cemetery is always worth checking during a fallout.

TLE

Seaside Sparrow

contains salt cedar, tallow, willow, and oak. Similar to the cemetery in Sabine Pass, the park is always worth checking during a fallout.

Continuing east on FM 3322 and turning right on South 1st takes you the 3.5 miles to the Pilot Station and Texas Point. The road to the Pilot Station is poorly maintained, so be prepared for a rough ride. Salt cedar hedges along this road can be remarkably productive during migration. After the passage of a late spring cold front, migrant landbirds such as vireos, warblers, tanagers, buntings, grosbeaks, and orioles abound. From winter through late spring, the cordgrass marshes bordering the

RAB/Naturewide Images

Nelson's Sharp-tailed Sparrow

FINDING NELSON'S SHARP-TAILED SPARROWS

The most habitat-specific of the grassland sparrows is Nelson's Sharp-tailed Sparrow. In East Texas it is not found outside of *Spartina* grass flats in tidally inundated salt marsh. Though it nests in the Great Plains, it is not seen in migration and can only be discovered once it has arrived in habitat on its wintering grounds. Texas Point, Anahuac, Yacht Basin Road, and Bolivar Flats are all good sites (25, 50, 57, and 58), and this sparrow responds fairly well to *pisshing* noises, as do the resident Seaside Sparrows with which it occurs. Sedge Wren and Le Conte's Sparrow may both be numerous in coastal habitats, but they avoid the tidally inundated saltmarsh inhabited by sharp-tailed sparrows. Note the sharp-tailed's white back streaks, not found in the similar grassland sparrows.

road support impressive numbers of Nelson's Sharp-tailed Sparrows. The larger and darker Seaside Sparrow is a year-round resident here. Watch for them scurrying along the margins of the tidal channels.

The road to Texas Point National Wildlife Refuge provides an excellent spot from which to look and listen for rails, wrens, and sparrows. The marshes are a great place to watch White Ibis feed and to marvel at the dexterity with which they use their awkward-looking pink saber bills to chase and extract food from the marsh mud.

Gray-cheeked Thrush

25: Texas Point National Wildlife Refuge

All Seasons
Free, Daily
Rating: 2
TX 87 2.4 miles W of Sabine Pass to Texas Point NWR; nature trail on south side of road.

If weather conditions are right, the stunted woods at the refuge can seethe with migrants. An interesting phenomenon on the coast is the uneven distribution of certain species. On some days, Sabine Woods may yield a nice show of Cerulean Warblers or Gray-cheeked Thrushes; Smith Oaks may get a couple of Blackpolls, while Boy Scout Woods will have none of these but may provide the day's only Golden-winged Warbler. Consequently, investigate all possible coastal woodlands. Sites like Texas Point can easily turn up the day's most treasured sighting. Recent nesting records for this small woodland include White-tailed Kite, Orchard Oriole, and Painted Bunting, so a peek during summer is never a waste of time.

Beyond the little stand of trees stretches the endless coastal marsh, a remarkable vista in its own right. Simply standing on the marsh and being aware of the vocalizations can be a powerful wildlife-watching experience. Early in the morning or later in the evening, rails and salt marsh specialties can be seen as well as heard. Nelson's Sharp-tailed Sparrow and Seaside Sparrow are generally lounging around the area, almost as if waiting for someone to watch them, and it can be quite a thrill if a shy and secretive rail emerges from the marsh grass for a brief parade.

26: Texas Ornithological Society Sabine Woods

Spring, Fall
Free, Daily
Rating: 3
TX 87 1.8 miles W of Texas Point NWR, entrance on right.

Swainson's Thrush

Thousands of birds, including water-birds, nightjars, and hummingbirds, make emergency landings on the Upper Texas Coast in spring after crossing the Gulf of Mexico, and a prime landing strip for them is Sabine Woods, particularly for the songbirds. The trees provide a perfect windbreak for birds that have had to battle storm fronts while migrating across the Gulf.

Upon entering the thicket, watch for trails leading to the left and right as well as trails around the western perimeter of the woods. Once inside, walk quietly. Notice that the visibility below the trees is quite good. Scan the ground well ahead for terrestrial species such as Swainson's, Kentucky, and Hooded warblers, Ovenbird, and *Catharus* thrushes. Follow any trill, buzz, or chip that does not immediately sound familiar. Migration is dynamic, and the birds come and go rapidly. Backtrack as often as necessary; a totally different selection of species may be present an hour later.

The ponds within the woods can be excellent for Louisiana Waterthrush (early migration), Northern Waterthrush (later), and Prothonotary Warbler. Sooner or later, almost everything comes to these ponds. By standing quietly near the water or sitting at the benches during the later afternoon, visitors will witness an impressive procession of thrashers, catbirds, thrushes, warblers, vireos, tanagers, orioles, and buntings that come in to bathe and drink. Check the pond behind the woods for Solitary Sandpiper, yellowlegs, ducks, and large waders.

During a fallout, or even during a particularly birdy afternoon, walk back to the parking area and scan southward over the water for small mixed flocks of songbirds that may have been traversing the Gulf nonstop for as long as sixteen hours. One after another, until it is too dark to see, migrants plummet out of the sky to rest, for fresh water, and to replenish their depleted energy reserves with insects. Viewing this spectacle drives home how much of the Texas coastline has been paved or otherwise developed for commerce and emphasizes the importance of protecting these few remaining coastal woodlands.

The Texas Ornithological Society (TOS), owner of the sanctuary, planted more than a hundred oak saplings. As these trees mature—many are well over head-high—this location becomes even more hospitable to birds. Do not discount a late summer or fall visit. Hundreds of Ruby-throated Hummingbirds may swarm the lantana thickets. The woods can be alive with *Empidonax* flycatchers, and western species such as Western Tanager and Black-headed Grosbeak have occurred here. At any time of

the year, look for Mottled Duck in the marsh across Texas Highway 87 from the sanctuary, which is part of the Texas Point NWR.

27: Sea Rim State Park

All Seasons
Site fee, Daily
Rating: 2
TX 87 4.8 miles W of TOS Sabine Woods to Sea Rim State Park; entrance on left. Marsh Unit north of TX 87 on right. Watch for boathouse at channel near parking area.

Named after a small native fish that is a voracious consumer of mosquitoes, the Gambusia Trail boardwalk east of the park headquarters offers an excellent view of marsh birds and waterbirds. Clapper Rails are plentiful in these marshes and are frequently

Willows at Sea Rim State Park

observed from the boardwalk. The beach supports impressive flocks of gulls, terns, and shorebirds. During winter scan well offshore for Greater and Lesser scaup and all three kinds of scoters. Along the boardwalk viewers stand an excellent chance of encountering a resident alligator. When the marsh is dry, ample evidence of alligator tracks remains.

The Gulf willows, salt cedars, and red mulberries growing along the southern edge of Texas Highway 87 are remarkably attractive to migrant landbirds; Cape May and Prairie warblers are regulars along this stretch of the coast. Local rarities such as eastern Bewick's Wren, eastern Palm Warbler, Bell's Vireo, and Black-throated Gray Warbler have occurred here, often lingering long enough for viewing by large numbers of people. During late summer and fall, migrating butterflies and dragonflies such as Monarch and Common Green Darner may be present by the thousands. The boardwalk alongside this woodland was built with funds provided by the Great Texas Coastal Birding Trail. The beach may be accessed at a number of points west on TX 87. Be sure to check the gull and tern flocks, because rarities such as Great Black-backed Gull, Lesser Black-backed Gull, and Glaucous Gull have been seen along this stretch of beach.

The Cave Swallows that nest under the eaves of the Sea Rim boathouse are perhaps the northernmost breeders on the Texas coast. Once relegated to relatively specific areas in West Texas, the Cave Swallow has experienced an explosive radiation owing mainly to new specifications for drainage culverts adopted in highway construction codes. These culverts, square in cross section, perfectly fit the needs for Cave Swallow nests and have provided a ready-made habitat combining the right sized "cave" and the right amount of rainfall for these birds to proliferate.

The state park, bordered by beach and salt marsh on one side and by a bay on the other, constitutes an impressively extensive habitat. It is one of the few places where there is freshwater marsh with large willow thickets and is in fact the largest willow grove in the area with public access. The extensive boardwalk was constructed to facilitate watching spring and fall migrants. The birding quality of the habitat is ephemeral; a wet spring or fall is preferable to the drier summer. After a good rain the marsh is transformed by the influx of water and the birdlife this attracts. Sea Rim State Park is also a wonderful stop because it is somewhat remote and consequently not likely to be crowded, especially in summer, when the temperature and humidity dissuade most visitors. The pleasant temperatures of late fall and winter make this strip of sandy coast an ideal retreat for anyone who wants some solitude, some natural beauty, and some fresh air.

28: McFaddin National Wildlife Refuge

All Seasons
Free, Daily
Rating: 2
From Sea Rim State Park Beach Unit, TX 87 W 1.9 miles to McFaddin NWR, 12.0 miles west of Sabine Pass.

McFaddin is primarily maintained for waterfowl. The gate closes at 3:00 P.M., so be sure to exit the area by then. The gravel road to Clam Lake offers prospects for a variety of wintering waterfowl, including the rare Masked Duck. Watch for migrating

raptors such as Merlin and Peregrine Falcon as well as for the locally uncommon Bobolink (spring) on or over the refuge marshes. Vermilion Flycatchers have occurred here from late fall through spring migration.

Just east of where you turn off Texas Highway 87 into the McFaddin refuge, a small boardwalk follows the Willow Pond Nature Trail. This short, convenient, beautiful little trail is an excellent spot to check for birds, especially if McFaddin is closed by the time you arrive. Red-winged Blackbirds are wont to fill the willows, which may give one a moment of reflection on the force that these fragile plants have to endure when hurricanes, tropical storms, and other violent squalls pile in from the Gulf of Mexico. Masked Duck, one of two North American stiff-tailed ducks, is an irruptive and irregular species in Texas. This bird occasionally occurs

RAB/Naturewide Images

Masked Duck

at McFaddin, so check carefully among the more common and very similar Ruddy Ducks.

29: J. D. Murphree Wildlife Management Area

All Seasons
Free, Daily
Rating: 2
From Sabine Pass, TX 87 N;
TX 82 N; TX 73 W 3.0 miles to J. D.
Murphree WMA.

Pass back over the bridge that spans Taylor Bayou, and about a quarter of a mile farther is a crossover that takes visitors a short distance up a dirt road. On the left are four large steel structures that look like silos. Immediately past them, on the left, is where the nature trail begins. Continuing straight, the road follows the levee and dead-ends at a building that abuts Taylor Bayou. The best way to experience the marsh is by boat. Texas Marshland Tours (409) 736-3023, a company that specializes in fishing charters, also conducts tours of the marsh for wildlife watchers.

The nature trail is one mile long, and early fall or late summer can produce Wood Stork and a host of other coastal marsh birds. At the end of the trail an observation deck gives an excellent view of the marsh and some of the smaller creeks that cut across the grassland.

J. D. Murphree WMA has diverse coastal wetland habitats in its three units: the Big Hill Unit, Lost Lake Unit, and Hillebrandt Unit. Habitats include freshwater, intermediate, and brackish marshes, with a few saline wetlands. The freshwater wetlands support an expanding association of exotic and noxious wetland plants; management spends considerable resources trying to control these introduced species. The Brown Pelican, Piping Plover, Louisiana black bear, and green, hawksbill, Kemp's Ridley, and loggerhead sea turtles have all been seen at this site.

Mottled Ducks breed and nest here, as do increasing numbers of Fulvous and Black-bellied Whistling-ducks,

RAB/Naturewide Images

Fulvous Whistling-Duck

Wood Stork

FINDING WOOD STORKS

Find this bird in late summer and fall. It breeds in Mexico and moves north after breeding, as does the Magnificent Frigatebird. Wood Stork flocks are usually seen in interior marshes such as those at the J. D. Murphree WMA, Anahuac National Wildlife Refuge (site 49), Davis Estates Road (see site 117), and Brazos Bend State Park (site 117). Look for an immense white and black stork feeding out in a wetland. An excellent place to scout for them in fall is the crawfish farming area on I-10 in Jefferson County. When farmers lower the pond water levels to harvest the crawfish, storks and innumerable Whimbrels fly in from miles around to snack on the exposed crustaceans.

in population rises that have been noted since the late 1980s. A large colonial waterbird rookery is located immediately west of Lost Lake Camp. Least Bittern is ubiquitous. Muskrat, nutria, swamp rabbit, eastern cottontail, raccoon, river otter, coyote, mink, opossum, armadillo, striped skunk, rice rat, white-footed mouse, bobcat, and cotton rat are some of the resident mammals at J. D. Murphree. The American alligator is the single most important reptile and predator here; J. D. Murphree has more than one alligator per acre, which is considered to be an extremely dense population.

This wildlife management area is the center of a small but important stopover and staging area for much of the waterfowl of the Central Flyway and provides high quality winter waterfowl habitat. The Chenier Plain marshes of Texas were once inhabited by the Atakapa Indians, and much of the J. D. Murphree WMA probably has high value for archaeological sites. Two such places have already been identified in the Big Hill Unit and on the shore of Hillebrandt Bayou.

30: Taylor Bayou

Spring, Summer
Free, Daily
Rating: 2
For South Fork: TX 73 W to Boondocks Road, N 1.2 miles to South Fork. *For North Fork:* Continue on Boondocks Road 1.4 miles to North Fork, then go on 1.0 mile to Patterson Road W for 1.2 miles; Craigen Road W goes 0.8 mile back to North Fork. *To reach Winnie:* Go an additional 2.4 miles on Craigen Road; TX 124 S 6.0 miles; TX 73 W 1.6.

Thousands of shorebirds may be in the rice fields along Texas Highway 73 in spring, especially in those that have recently been flooded. Many of the eastern Pineywoods inhabitants are present here, so this site—ecologically a finger of Big Thicket habitat extending downward into the coastal plain—provides a good chance to pick up species such as Broad-winged and Red-shouldered hawks as well as a nesting Swallow-tailed Kite. Northern Parula and Yellow-throated, Prothonotary, Swainson's, Kentucky, and Hooded warblers all breed in the vicinity. Few places along the upper coast are more reliable for Barred Owls.

Taking Boondocks Road to the T-junction with Burrell-Wingate Road, see good stands of roadside hardwoods that can be productive. There is little traffic on these roads, but take care not to block the right-of-way. Near the bayou all the homes are built on stilts. Taylor Bayou tends to rise after heavy rains; take care going through water on the road after a storm.

Alan Murphy, www.AlanMurphyPhotography.com

Prothonotary Warbler

FINDING PROTHONOTARY WARBLERS

This is one of only two hole-nesting warblers in North America, often using Downy Woodpecker cavities in the willows and cypresses of wooded swamps. Its loud and piercing song—a series of repeated notes—is usually heard well before the bird is seen. Find the bird by *pisshing* and squeaking. Taylor Bayou, Brazos Bend State Park (site 117), all waterways of the Big Thicket, bridges across wooded sloughs, and Martin Dies Jr. State Park (site 13) are likely to produce this bird. It also abounds in the coastal migrant traps.

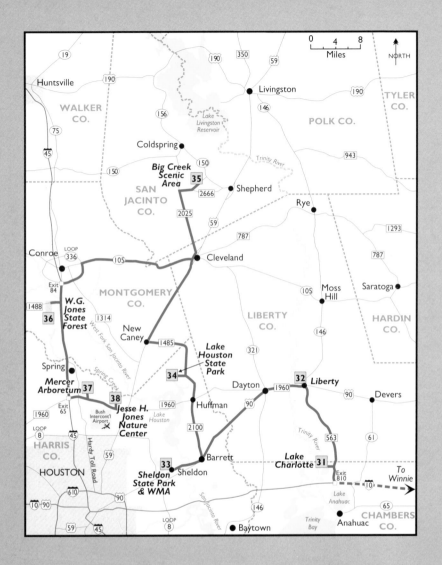

Trinity Loop

Some sites on the Trinity Loop are set in a suburban area and represent an oasis of flowers, trees, butterflies, and birds. For birders on a tight schedule, or those who are based in the Greater Houston metropolitan area—especially the northern part near George Bush Intercontinental Airport—the Trinity Loop is unquestionably the best bet for good variety in birding and a chance to experience the woodlands of East Texas. For in-transit birders who have a layover at George the airport, Trinity Loop site 36 offers a quick and convenient venue for viewing the endangered Red-cockaded Woodpecker. The Trinity Loop also includes three sites that have child-friendly facilities. The botanical garden at Mercer Arboretum, the environmental education center at Sheldon State Park, and the Jesse H. Jones Nature Center all provide a greater variety of activities that may appeal to children than do most other sites.

The Trinity River floodplain includes a number of diverse wetland habitats: bottomland hardwood forests, wooded swamps, open water, and wet pastures. Upland areas outside the floodplain contain cultivated pastures, natural pine forests, and mixed pine-hardwood forests. The Trinity River National Wildlife Refuge and lands surrounding it that have been proposed for acquisition provide important breeding, wintering, and stopover habitat for numerous species of waterfowl and neotropical migrants. A total of 275 species of birds occurs in the bottomland forests and associated wetlands in eastern Texas; 100 bird species are known or believed to breed here. Of interest to naturalists, the Trinity River NWR is home to more than 600 plant species and more than 400 kinds of vertebrates.

©Natalie Wiest

Canoers on Lake Charlotte

31: Lake Charlotte
All Seasons
Free, Daily
Rating: 1
From Winnie, I-10 W; FM 563 N 2.8 miles; Lake Charlotte Road W 1.3 miles to the lake.

Northern Parula and Yellow-throated, Prothonotary, Swainson's, and Hooded warblers are common from late spring through summer. This site can be good for Wood Stork, and postbreeders from southeastern Mexico may appear by the hundreds. Look for them during summer and early fall. Much of the lakeside is paralleled by a wide trail and lake access points. A drive along Lake Charlotte Road can turn up woodland species such as Barred Owl, Eastern Screech-Owl, and Pileated Woodpecker along the more densely wooded sections.

For those who have a canoe or kayak, there are places along the Trinity River to put in and bird by boat. Most impressive are the dense stands of cypress that line the lake. The "deep woods, big thicket" feel once characteristic of this entire region still exists here. Bald Eagles nest in this area, a symbol of coordinated conservation efforts coalescing to save a species. The cypress swamp bordering Lake Charlotte is the most impressive example of this habitat remaining on the Upper Texas Coast.

32: Liberty

All Seasons
Free, Daily
Rating: 2
From I-10, FM 563 N 14.5 miles; US 90 to Liberty. From US 90 in Dayton, FM 1409 S 10.5 miles to County Road 417, left for 1.8 miles to Trinity River NWR Champion Lake.

Although there is a Great Texas Coastal Birding Trail sign upon entering Liberty, the actual turn toward the municipal park cannot be seen until the stoplight at the McDonald's. Turn right at the golden arches and go for about a mile. There is a small shopping center on the left and a stoplight; turn left here and go straight into the city park.

The park consists primarily of recreational fields, but a jogging trail borders some nice stands of hardwood that include maple and oak (and some Chinese tallow, an invasive exotic that consumes considerable time and resources in attempts to limit its spread). During spring and summer, Prothonotary Warblers will

Stuart Marcus, U.S. Fish & Wildlife Service

Trinity River National Wildlife Refuge Champion Lake

likely be flitting around among the foliage.

To reach the Liberty flood-control levee road, go back toward downtown and turn right onto Monta Street; there is a Pantry Foods on the corner. Little parking is available on the levee road, and in the morning the road can be crowded with buses unloading at the high school. While birding along the river in summer, watch for a Swallow-tailed Kite soaring overhead. These birds nest in the area. The Trinity River itself serves as a vector for migrants. During spring and fall, be sure to check the skies for migrating hawks.

The Trinity River National Wildlife Refuge, established in 1994 by the U.S. Fish and Wildlife Service, includes an eight-hundred-acre public use area at Champion Lake and affords an excellent opportunity to bird the bottomland forests. The pier at the lake makes a good observation deck, and from May until September Swallow-tailed Kites are the main attraction. Birders will also see ducks, waders, Bald Eagle, Osprey, Wood Stork, Painted Bunting, Vermilion Flycatcher, Eastern Bluebird, and many species of warblers, depending on the time of year. The refuge has several trails open to the public, but because this is bottomland habitat, these trails flood and can get wet and muddy. There is a portable toilet at Champion Lake but no other facilities.

The refuge's Web site offers the latest information and its USFWS office is on North Main Street in Liberty, open 8 A.M. to 4 P.M., Monday through Friday.

With a number of bed-and-breakfasts and traditional lodging, Liberty is well situated to serve as a base from which to bird this intriguing region of Texas.

33: Sheldon Lake State Park and Sheldon Wildlife Management Area

Migrations, Winter
Site fee, Daily
Rating: 2
Park headquarters is at 15315 Beaumont Hwy (Business 90), 2 miles E of Beltway 8 or 2 miles W of Sheldon Rd at PR 138.

The swamp habitat at Sheldon is superb. Ibis, hawks, and a plethora of waterbirds abound here. A bit of luck may produce Purple Gallinule. Woodcocks winter in the damp understory and display at dusk in the late winter and early spring.

The willow, cypress, and water lilies at Sheldon are beautiful, and the environmental learning center has a garden that demonstrates xeriscaping techniques, native flora landscaping, and techniques for developing butterfly and hummingbird gardens; it

Purple Gallinule (immature)

RAB/Naturewide Images

34: Lake Houston Park

Migrations, Winter
Site fee, Daily
Rating: 2
From US 90 FM 2100 N 22.7 miles;
FM 2100 veers west and becomes
FM 1485; Baptist Encampment Road
S 1.6 miles to park.

Formerly a state park, Lake Houston Park is now the property of the Houston Parks and Recreation Department (HPRD). HPRD is in the process of renovating the facilities at the park, and over the next few years this park should offer an enhanced experience. Lake Houston Park is a good venue for breeding birds that include Carolina Wren, Yellow-billed Cuckoo, Red-eyed, Yellow-throated and White-eyed vireos, Hooded and Kentucky warblers, and Summer Tanager. Henslow's Sparrows are

also has fishing ponds with a number of alligators. Little Blue Heron may be seen around the ponds.

Sheldon Lake State Park and Sheldon WMA are most productive in winter, with flocks of gulls, terns, and waterfowl blanketing the various lakes and ponds. The surrounding weedy fields often hold Sedge Wrens and a variety of sparrows. Look carefully for the secretive Le Conte's Sparrow.

RAB/Naturewide Images

Summer Tanager

found in winter in the grasslands along utility rights-of-way, and look for Osprey around the cypress-lined lakes. Campsites are available at the park, and because of its proximity to several urban and suburban areas, this park can be crowded during weekends.

The park is also an excellent site for dragonflies. Pay particular attention to the numerous species of skimmers that inhabit the edge of the lake. During sunny, windless days, the banks can be thick with a variety of colorful dragonflies. Added bonuses, as with most of the sites on the Trinity Loop, are proximity to Houston and habitat that is deeper and more wooded than the sites near Humble and FM 1960. Lake Houston Park is bigger, more extensive, more varied, and farther removed from the urbanized areas of north Houston.

35: Big Creek Scenic Area

Migrations, Winter
Free, Daily
Rating: 2
From Cleveland on US 59, FM 2025 N 10.0 miles; FM 2666 E 2.5 miles; FS (Forest Service Rd) 221 0.5 mile; FS 217 E 0.9 mile to Big Creek Scenic Area.

This site is somewhat difficult to find but well worth the trouble. Big Creek is a famous stop for butterflies and dragonflies. Significant research has been conducted here, and it is not uncommon to find biologists observing insects in the area. Pileated Woodpecker, Hairy Woodpecker (occasional), Acadian Flycatcher, Wood Thrush, Worm-eating Warbler, and Louisiana Waterthrush nest here. The area also provides habitat for large numbers of Hooded Warblers, dynamic birds to see with their brilliant coloration and bright song. Big Creek is almost always birdy, scenic, and a good choice if time is a factor. Kentucky Warbler and Swainson's Warbler occur here in spring and summer.

Interesting and sparsely distributed aquatic insects such as Sely's Sundragon and Laura's Clubtail (both rare Texas dragonflies) have been observed in this area, as have Phantom Craneflies: small black-and-white-banded insects that fly very slowly close to the ground and then become invisible just as the viewer becomes aware of their presence. These insects haunt the trail that passes east from the parking lot toward the creek. This portion of San Jacinto County hosts over ninety species of dragonflies and damselflies, about twice the total for the British Isles. During early spring, look for the large Gray Petaltail (frequently referred to as a living fossil) on tree trunks near the parking area. These attractive insects frequently use people as hunting perches and are,

Falcate Orangetip

of course, harmless. Butterflies are abundant; early spring specialties include Falcate Orangetip, Eastern Pine and Henry's elfins, and Spring Azure.

36: W. G. Jones State Forest

All Seasons
Free, Daily
Rating: 2
From Cleveland TX 105 W 18.7 miles; Loop 336 S 5.5 miles; I-45 S 3.0 miles; FM 1488 W 1.4 miles to state forest. From George Bush Intercontinental Airport, take Loop 8 E to I-45, N to FM 1488 as above.

Birders interested in ornithological history may want to detour east about twenty miles to where Texas Highway 105 intersects Gaylor Creek and Gaylor Lake. It was at this site, in November of 1904, that Vernon Bailey shot the last two Ivory-billed Woodpeckers in Texas. This forest has one of the state's densest concentrations of endangered Red-cockaded Woodpeck-

Yellow-bellied Sapsucker

ers. It also hosts an excellent variety of other woodpeckers, including Pileated, Red-headed, Downy, Hairy, and Red-bellied woodpeckers, Northern Flicker, and Yellow-bellied Sapsucker.

Do not be surprised to find people from all over the world at this out-of-the-way spot. France, Belgium, Great Britain, Germany, Japan, and a host of other countries are well represented among visitors to this site, which serves as a gathering point for birders passing through George Bush Intercontinental Airport who want to see a Red-cockaded Woodpecker. W. G. Jones State Forest is about a forty-minute drive from Intercontinental, and for the birder just passing through from Europe or Asia, this is the closest venue for viewing the woodpecker.

Accessible woodpecker groups include one reached by a marked trail behind the Forest Service office and another south of FM 1488 at Middle Lake, although this site is sometimes closed. Middle Lake may be reached by turning south for 2.3 miles west of Interstate 10 on Jones Road, a dead-end dirt road. This turnoff is easy to overshoot. Drive south a very short distance, then turn left to the lakefront with picnic tables, yard ducks, and parking areas on both sides of the access road. At the far end of the right-hand parking lot is a

RAB/Naturewide Images

Palamedes Swallowtail

broad, marked trail to the right that continues several hundred yards southward to Middle Lake. Check first at the headquarters building to see if areas on the south side of the road are open. All Red-cockaded Woodpecker nest trees are marked with green bands painted around the trunks. Many nest openings are lined with artificial inserts. Do not disturb these birds by playing tapes or knocking on the painted cavity trees; it is a felony.

In spring, azaleas at the headquarters may be covered with Palamedes Swallowtails. Superior loblolly, sweetgum, and dense understory around the forest provide excellent habitat for a variety of birds. For the botanically inclined, a pamphlet is available to help identify plants in these managed woodlands.

Other birds in the forest or along its open margins may include Wood Duck, Green Heron, Yellow-crowned Night-Heron, Great Horned Owl, Eastern Screech-Owl, Barred Owl, Chuck-will's-widow, Broad-winged Hawk, Acadian and Great Crested flycatchers, Eastern Bluebird, Carolina Wren, Brown-headed Nuthatch, Blue-gray Gnatcatcher, Carolina Chickadee, and Tufted Titmouse; Blue-headed, White-eyed, and Yellow-throated vireos; Yellow-rumped and Pine warblers; and Summer Tanager and Painted Bunting. Listen for the high-pitched chitter of the Brown-headed Nuthatch, a bird limited to the southeastern United States and a target species for many visitors to this part of Texas.

This forest has produced approximately fifty species of damselflies and dragonflies, including the locally rare Amanda's Pennant, Plains Clubtail, and Vesper Bluet. Species such as Swamp Spreadwing that are found around Middle Lake are not necessarily represented at the front lake adjacent to FM 1488. Early spring populations are decidedly different from later assemblages and, as with birds, this site can be visited numerous times before one has a full sense of its species potential.

37: Mercer Arboretum and Botanical Gardens

All Seasons
Free, Daily
Rating: 1
From I-45 N of George Bush Intercontinental Airport take FM 1960 E; Aldine-Westfield Road N 1.1 miles to arboretum on left.

Except for site 38, this is the closest birding venue to Houston's George Bush Intercontinental Airport. Birders with limited time who are in Houston for a business meeting or conference find this a convenient, easily accessible site. The arboretum has hard-

RAB/Naturewide Images

Migrant Monarchs

woods and dense understory mixed with pine, and it showcases Texas native plants in a 250-acre habitat, including wildflowers, carnivorous plants, and endangered species. One of the easiest places to view migrating Monarch butterflies is at Mercer Arboretum, where large numbers of the estimated 100 million butterflies that make their way through Texas during the month of October can be seen. The Monarch is one of only a handful of local butterfly species that migrates and the only long-distance migrating butterfly in North America. Miles of nature trails, a butterfly nursery, koi ponds, picnic areas, and guided tours also are available at the arboretum.

38: Jesse H. Jones Nature Center

All Seasons
Free, Daily
Rating: 1
From I-45 N of Bush Intercontinental Airport take FM 1960 E 5.1 miles beyond Aldine-Westfield Road (turnoff to arboretum, site 37); Kenswick Road N 1.2 miles through housing development to nature center.

Trails meander through moist forest and past ponds margined with bald cypress, eventually reaching the banks of Spring Creek. Among local birders, this park is best known for nesting Swainson's Warblers, but newcomers to the area will find an

FINDING RED-COCKADED WOODPECKERS

Look for this species in the morning, when individuals are actively feeding. These chatty birds are fairly easy to find when they are out and about. Spring—when the pairs are noisy, more active, and preparing to nest—is perhaps the best season in which to find them. The red "cockade," a tiny dot below the crown, is almost invisible in the field. This bird is best distinguished from the some-what similar Hairy Wood-pecker by a distinct, large white cheek area, coarse white barring along the back, and spotted or barred pat-terning along the sides and flanks. The bird's tapping or short, high-pitched *preet* calls often indicate its location.

Greg W. Lasley/KAC Productions

Red-cockaded Woodpecker

Eastern Screech-Owl

abundance of common eastern forest species as well. The park supports populations of both Eastern Screech-Owls and Barred Owls but is closed to the public at night. Leaders of organized field trips who wish to schedule an owl prowl are asked to telephone ahead and make arrangements with the park manager.

Continue east on FM 1960 to U.S. Highway 90 and Texas Highway 146 in Dayton, and go south on TX 146 to Interstate 10. Tundra Swan, which is very rare along the upper coast, has been seen in winter along this drive.

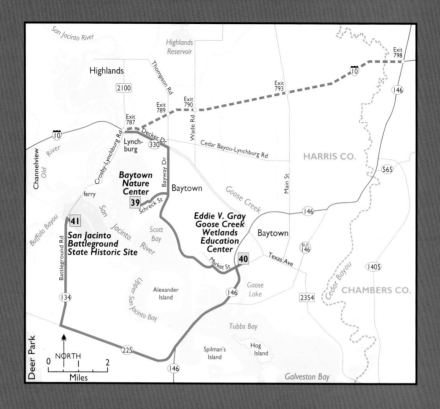

San Jacinto River

Highlands
Reservoir

Thompson Rd

Highlands
2100

Exit 798

10

146

Exit 793

Exit 790

Exit 789

Exit 787

Wade Rd

10

Channelview

Decker Dr

Lynch-
burg

Cedar Bayou-Lynchburg Rd

HARRIS CO.

565

330

Crosby-Lynchburg Rd

Bayway Dr

Baytown Nature Center

39

Baytown

Goose Creek

Main St

146

ferry

Schreck St

San

Jacinto

River

41

San Jacinto Battleground State Historic Site

Scott Bay

Eddie V. Gray Goose Creek Wetlands Education Center

Baytown

Old River

Buffalo Bayou

Battleground Rd

134

Upper San Jacinto Bay

Alexander Island

Market St

40

Texas Ave

BUS 146

146

Goose Lake

1405

CHAMBERS CO.

2354

225

Tubbs Bay

Spilman's Island

Hog Island

146

Galveston Bay

Deer Park

NORTH

0   1   2

Miles

San Jacinto Loop

The three sites on the San Jacinto Loop offer some of the last existing tidal marshland habitat in the region, a reclaimed wetland on the site of a sunken subdivision that was itself originally reclaimed marshland. This is surely one of the rare cases in the Americas where a housing subdivision raised on wetland habitat has been taken back by the swamp. A wetlands education center that provides both opportunities to watch wildlife and a physical structure for community nature education outreach programs can be found here.

This modest complex of sites is invitingly close to the Houston metroplex and has the added advantage that an early morning trip goes against the flow of traffic, and the return in the evening does, too.

39: Baytown Nature Center

All
Site fee, Daily
Rating: 1
From intersection of TX 146 and I-10,
I-10 W 9.3 miles; Crosby-Lynchburg Road/Spur 330 1.3 miles; Bayway Drive S 1.4 miles; Shreck W 1.0 mile to site of nature center.

There is a four-way stop intersection with a bait shop on the right at the Crosby-Lynchburg exit from Interstate 10. If you turn right here, the road leads to the Lynchburg ferry landing, where the ferry crosses the Houston Ship Channel to San Jacinto Battleground–Battleship *Texas* State Historic Site (site 41, later on this loop); the roadside leading to the ferry is worth checking for birds before you head for the Baytown Nature Center. To reach the nature center, go straight across at the four-way stop, continue for almost 1.5 miles, and turn right at the first traffic light. There is no sign, but this is Bayway Drive. Continue down Bayway past the junior high school, and after about one and a half miles pass Beeper's on the right. The next street is Schreck; note the birding trail sign on the corner. Turn right on Shreck and follow it to the entrance.

This site is a former subdivision

Roseate Spoonbill (juvenile)

RAB/Naturewide Images

that sank due to land subsidence resulting from the pumping of groundwater out of the water table beneath Baytown. There are still numerous remnants of the subdivison, but on the whole it has been returned to nature and the habitat now consists of mesquite, salt cedar, and extensive coastal marsh, where over three hundred species of birds have occurred. Sandpipers feed in the muddy pools; Roseate Spoonbills, Ospreys, egrets and herons, swallows, dragonflies, and butterflies abound. Wood Storks often feed in these marshes in late summer and fall; the flocks of herons, egrets, and spoonbills are present all year.

At San Jacinto Point the city has created new marsh areas, erected two observation towers, and built a parking area partly funded by a federal Coastal Management Program grant. Other improvements throughout the nature center's 450 acres include new walking trails, three fishing piers, two pavilions, new picnic sites, the Crystal Bay Butterfly Garden, a selectively planted songbird habitat, and a new freshwater lake. Visitors may be startled—even repulsed—by the surrounding landscape of petrochemical refineries. That so much land here has been rendered biologically sterile highlights the importance of Galveston Bay's few enhanced and protected sites.

40: Eddie V. Gray Wetlands Education and Recreation Center

All Seasons
Free, Daily
Rating: 1
From TX 146, Market Street E to Wetlands Center, (281) 420-7128.

This center, situated on the banks of Goose Creek, is an excellent complement to the previous site, which is a wildlife management area. The display section of the center is a converted bowling alley, and many of the exhibits have been built with the help of donations from the Rotary Club, Bayer, and ExxonMobil. The science room has a full complement of micro-scopes, and the center cycles about fifteen hundred fifth graders through its doors each week for a variety of educational programs. This site provides indoor informational materials and is particularly recommended for children. Look for Black-crowned Night-Heron and various shorebirds in the small wetland behind the center.

RAB./Naturewide Images

Black-crowned Night-Heron

RAB/Naturewide Images

Red-breasted Merganser

41: San Jacinto Battleground–Battleship *Texas* State Historic Site

Migrations, Winter
Free, Daily
Rating: 2
From TX 146, TX 225 E 2.1 miles; TX 134/Battleground Road N 0.9 mile; Park Road 1836 leads to park.

The ponds here attract a variety of gulls, terns, waders, and water-fowl. Wood Storks can be spotted in late summer and fall, and Hooded Mergansers and Greater Scaup in winter.

Unlike Red-breasted Merganser, which is relatively easy to see on the Texas coast in winter, Hooded Merganser is much harder to find. This site is near the southern end of the bird's wintering grounds, and although uncommon in general, it is often found on the lakes below the San Jacinto Monument. The marsh at San Jacinto Battleground forms an important component of the battleground and is noteworthy as the last remaining tidal marsh in the area. Tidal marsh restoration began in 1996 with the help of the Texas Parks and Wildlife Department, federal agencies, and the private sector.

Construction of containment levees and reshaping the bottom so that it would support emergent vegetation were the principal means by which the marsh was restored. Sediments dredged during maintenance of the Houston Ship Channel were used to bring the bottom to the right depth for the marsh. Marsh cordgrass was planted by hand, and other wetland vegetation has spread rapidly. This site's appeal should increase with time as the vegetation matures and invertebrate populations increase.

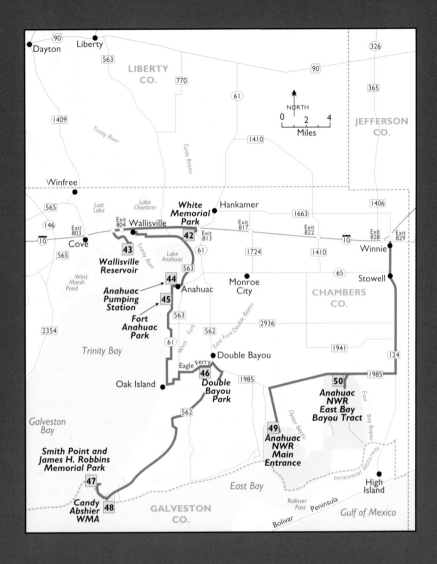

Anahuac Loop

This loop includes the Anahuac National Wildlife Refuge, one of the most important sites for wildlife viewing on the Upper Texas Coast. The rest of the sites on the loop are much smaller, but together they create a mosaic of venues that, when birded as a unit, stand to produce an excellent cross section of birdlife. Although the refuge commands a significant amount of time for anyone who wants to explore it in depth, many of the smaller sites can be visited in a few minutes, depending on the amount of bird activity. Spring migration is a dynamic event that can turn a quiet county park into a riot of neotropical migrants; no venue should be overlooked at this time of year.

This entire area was once prone to sheet-flooding, and prior to flood control residents got around by boat during the rainy season. Anahuac's richness in animal and plant life is noteworthy at numerous sites along this loop.

Anahuac is a superb waterfowl refuge and is good for birding during every single month of the year. In summer, sites on the Anahuac Loop may provide views of bobcats, alligators, river otters, and nutria. The charismatic nature of these animals makes this area of particular interest to children as well, since they can safely get intimate views of diverse animals, especially alligators. From late spring to late fall visitors should be prepared for high heat and humidity as well as mosquitoes and, as summer progresses, biting flies.

The precarious status of the rice economy is of tremendous importance to the hundreds of thousands of shorebirds that pause during their northbound migration to feed in flooded rice fields, including American Golden-Plover, Whimbrel, Hudsonian Godwit, Long-billed Dowitcher, and Semipalmated, Western, Baird's, and White-rumped sandpipers. Although none of these fields is designated as a site on the loop, visitors should watch the numerous flooded fields with vigilance for the shorebirds that alight here.

The most convenient lodgings for birding Lake Charlotte, Anahuac, Smith Point, High Island, and the area's many rice fields are in High

Rice stubble

Island, Winnie, and (although less direct) at Crystal Beach to the west on the Bolivar Peninsula. Some High Island residents rent rooms to visitors during spring migration. Virtually all lodging is booked up months prior to spring migration. Because of this and the scarcity of restaurants available at what may be the country's most popular springtime birding venue, most birders elect to stay along I-10 in Winnie, or, if they want to be closer to the Big Thicket as well, in Beaumont.

42: White Memorial Park

Migrations, Summer
Free, Daily
Rating: 1
From I-10, TX 61 S 0.2 mile, turn right into White Memorial Park.

The birding trail sign for White Memorial Park seems to come and go, but the park is fairly easy to see from Texas Highway 61. Turtle Bayou, which runs along the edge of the park, is beautiful. The cypresses along the bayou edge and the stands of sweetgum and oak combine to

Prince Baskettail

produce a pleasing woodland birding area that becomes especially active in the evening hours. The trees are typically alive with woodpeckers, although park management in recent years has tended to cut down snags and has consequently reduced the park's attractiveness to these birds.

As it arcs through the park, the entrance road passes picnic tables and campsites, eventually depositing visitors back on TX 61 to continue south toward Anahuac NWR, Smith Point, and High Island. Although it has been battered by a series of hurricanes that destroyed many fine old trees, the park's remaining pines, magnolias, sweetgums, and the dense surround-ing understory host a representative selection of eastern woodland birds. Pileated, Downy, Red-bellied, and Red-headed woodpeckers nest here and on the road roughly opposite the park entrance. Hairy Woodpeckers prefer to nest in freshly killed trees. Yellow-crowned Night-Heron, Barred Owl, Great Crested and Acadian flycatchers, Carolina Wren, Carolina Chickadee, Pine Warbler, Hooded Warbler, and Summer Tanager are among the species that nest in the park and the surrounding forest. Take particular care to search the ground in the damper, wooded areas along the creek. Swainson's Warbler, while rare, could occur at this park. Watch for Eastern Bluebird near the stables at the north end of the park. During spring, watch also for Prince Basket-tail flitting over the bayou—our only very large, continuously airborne dragonfly with patterned wings. During much of the year, the tiny orange Eastern Amberwing—one of the only North American dragonflies that displays to attract a female—may be seen here as well.

43: Wallisville Reservoir

All Seasons
Free, Daily
Rating: 2
I-10 W, cross Trinity River bridge, and immediately exit. Turn back east toward river on service road, continue under bridge to Wallisville Reservoir West Levee Marsh. Accessible on foot only. Return to I-10 E 1.0 mile, recross river, and take exit 806. Loop back west on service road to river and Trinity River Mouth Waterbird Rookery immediately to the south. Return to I-10 E 1.1 miles to Levee Road and Wallisville Reservoir East Levee, the public access point for the reservoir. *To Horseshoe Ponds Trail*: Continue east from exit 807 at Wallisville, cross under freeway, then return west on north service road for approximately 0.5 mile.

Black-necked Stilt

For visitors coming from Houston, this site should be visited before site 42 to avoid backtracking. The Trinity River Mouth Waterbird Rookery, adjoining this site, is closed from February until June. Previously appreciated only at highway speeds but now viewable from a platform, the rookery is spectacular. Look for Anhinga, White Ibis, and Roseate Spoonbill in the area. Black-necked Stilts, egrets, herons, ducks, ibis, and a plethora of shorebirds all occur here. A natural blind at the edge of the mudflat consists of beautiful cypress draped with moss. Peering out from the cypress cover at the quacking ducks and feeding waterbirds, the experience of gazing out unobserved on this wildlife spectacle is wonderful. Morning is the best time to be at the rookery because the sun comes up from the far end of the mudflat and creates truly amazing lighting effects over the water and trees. Excellent opportunities for morning photography are available at this site.

44: Anahuac Pumping Station

All Seasons
Free, Daily
Rating: 1
On TX 61. From Wallisville Reservoir East Levee, Levee Road S 0.3 mile; Wallisville-Turtle Bayou Road E 3.4 miles; FM 563 S 5.6 miles; TX 61 W 0.9 mile to pumping station.

A birding trail along the levee road is lined with willow, mesquite, and salt cedar and attracts both migratory and nesting songbirds. Terns and kingfishers await visitors who walk the path. The diversity of aquatic habitats—freshwater and brackish marsh, and the open water of both bay and lake—means that any number of interesting birds could occur here. Watch for nesting Purple Gallinules, large waders such as Roseate Spoonbills, a variety of shorebirds, and wintering sparrows. Check the woodlands during migration.

45: Fort Anahuac Park

Migrations
Free, Daily
Rating: 2
From TX 61, South Main S 1.1 miles to park.

Fort Anahuac is a woodland park with a long levee road that follows the mouth of the Trinity River where it empties into Trinity Bay, a portion of the Galveston Bay system. A host

Great Egret

of terns, gulls, and egrets may be enjoyed here as well as a good assortment of sparrows that pop in and out of the marsh grass. Trees in the park provide cover and forage for spring neotropical migrants and should be checked carefully, particularly after a late-season cold front.

46: Double Bayou Park

Migrations
Free, Daily
Rating: 1
From TX 61, Eagle Ferry Road E 2.8 miles to park on right.

Double Bayou Park's mixed stands of pine and hardwood provide a potential landing zone for spring migrants, particularly after inclement weather. Watch for up to half a dozen species of woodpeckers and for birds typical of these moist forests, such as Brown Thrasher, White-eyed and Red-eyed vireos, Hooded and Pine warblers, Northern Parula, Eastern Wood-Pewee, and Indigo Bunting. Early or late visits may produce Yellow-crowned Night-Herons hunting crawfish in the park's more open habitat.

RAB/Naturewide Images

Brown Thrasher

RAB/Naturewide Images

Magnificent Frigatebird (immature)

47: Smith Point and James H. Robbins Memorial Park

All Seasons
Free, Daily
Rating: 2
From TX 61, Eagle Ferry Road E 3.1 miles; FM 562 S 1.0 mile; after junction with FM 1985, continue on FM 562 veering west 14.3 miles; Smith Point Road W 0.7 mile; Hawkins Camp Road 1.8 miles to Robbins Memorial Park.

This site is a popular put-in for fishermen and has a nice observation tower in the parking area from which to view sand spits in the bay that are frequented by gulls and terns. A spotting scope significantly improves the number of viewable birds. The Magnificent Frigatebird occurs here in summer and early fall; by October or November it becomes quite rare and is usually absent in winter.

Check the marshes and open grasslands along FM 562 irrespective of season. In winter look for Savannah and Swamp sparrows and scan the fruiting wax myrtles for huge swarms of Tree Swallows that feed on the bluish berries.

Swainson's Hawk

48: Candy Abshier Wildlife Management Area

Migrations (especially fall), Winter
Free, Daily
Rating: 3
See site 47 directions; return to Smith Point Road and go W 1.0 mile to wildlife management area.

During fall migration this site is a must. Birds migrating southward, especially birds of prey, concentrate along this peninsula before crossing Galveston Bay. Note that at this time, the area cannot be accessed via the road where the Great Texas Coastal Birding Trail sign is posted. Rather, continue straight along Smith Point Road and turn left into the entrance indicated by a sign for the hawk observation tower and for hawk tours.

The Candy Abshier Wildlife Management Area is one of the state's premier sites for fall hawk watching. The high observation tower provides unobstructed views of migrating raptors that can number from the dozens to the tens of thousands. The presence of other birders during the annual Hawk Watch provides visitors with ample opportunity to exchange information with like-minded naturalists. Raptors that are typically seen flying alone are even more impressive when seen in vast flocks. Check the vicinity for Swainson's Hawk, which spends the night standing in plowed fields. With luck, hundreds can be seen in one place, providing ample opportunity to look at diverse plumage types within a single species.

Hawk watches increase one's chance of seeing rare birds, which concentrate at migratory bottlenecks just as other species do. Consider the Swallow-tailed Kite: more of these birds are seen from the observation platform at Candy Abshier WMA each year than the total nesting population in Texas. Birders also get to see other locally rare birds of prey because of the landform features that funnel the birds into this migration corridor.

This site is a bonanza for other migrating creatures as well. Songbirds (including Scissor-tailed Flycatchers, Dickcissels, and Indigo Buntings), dragonflies, Monarch butterflies, mixed flocks of Wood Storks and Anhingas, pelicans, and Ruby-throated Hummingbirds all come through in large numbers. The oaks on the WMA can be very productive for migrants in spring, and rarities such as Henslow's Sparrow have been recorded in the nearby grassy fields.

49: Anahuac National Wildlife Refuge, Main Entrance

All Seasons
Free, Daily
Rating: 3

From I-10, TX 124 S, E on FM 1985 to main entrance, then 3 miles to refuge headquarters.

Anahuac National Wildlife Refuge is among the premier stops on the Great Texas Coastal Birding Trail. During spring the interpretive center operated by the Friends of Anahuac Refuge provides additional literature, directions, patches, T-shirts and other birding accoutrements. Washrooms are opposite the kiosk, and behind it is a pond that is seasonally alive with shorebirds and several species of dragonflies. There is no drinking water on the refuge (cold drinks may be purchased when the interpretive center is open), and the use of tapes for attracting birds on the refuge is prohibited.

RAB/Naturewide Images

Seaside Dragonlet

A recently installed pond and butterfly garden adjacent to the interpretive center provide natural history experiences as soon as you park your car. Friends of Anahuac Refuge and volunteers have been responsible for numerous improvements at the refuge, a testament to the effectiveness of grassroots concern about the environment.

Anahuac NWR was established for waterfowl and also for the remaining vestige of a red wolf population that has now hybridized with coyotes. The management plan for the refuge includes planting trees (a rare commodity in coastal grasslands) in order to provide more cover and forage for migrating songbirds. This habitat diversification provides important living space for birds that are under pressure from development all along the Texas coast.

Before leaving the interpretive center area, scan the wires for Scissor-tailed Flycatcher, Eastern Kingbird, and Purple Martin (spring to late summer), as well as for resident Loggerhead Shrikes. Park at the willow-lined pond north of the levee, which is known by local birders as "The Willows." This is an excellent spot for spring and fall migrants such as orioles, tanagers, grosbeaks, and many species of warblers, including the eastern Palm Warbler. Check these trees in late August and September for *Empidonax* flycatchers and warblers.

The water hyacinth–covered slough adjacent to the pond frequently hosts Sora and occasionally King Rail or Least Bittern. Watch for alligators and cottonmouths. In this area, too, listen for the flat, nasal *aaaaaaaaaaaa* of the pear-shaped, inch-long eastern narrow-mouthed frog.

The road around the pond is a one-way loop. Fringing vegetation height varies with water level and burn regimes, making visibility variable. Often the best views are near the northwest corner of the pond around the observation ramp. In winter, carefully check the mixed flocks of Greater White-fronted Geese and Snow Geese in the marshes and wet fields. Look for the smaller, shorter-necked, stubby-billed Ross's Goose, often interspersed in small numbers with Snow Geese.

Both sides of the road along the first straight stretch (the northern edge of the pond) are good for summering Least Bittern, an abundant breeder. Listen for the soft *co-co-co-co-co* and watch for the bird's tiny form a few inches above the surface of the water, where it often clings to reeds. Here too, especially on sunny days, look for the American alligator. The refuge hosts many fine, large specimens; do not approach or feed them. Despite the fact that most individuals appear to be resting, the alligator can be a tremendously dynamic

RAB/Naturewide Images

Nutria

animal to watch and photograph. Males display by lifting themselves out of the water and taking a deep breath, and as they lower themselves they let out a tremendously loud bellowing noise. Watch also for mammals including white-tailed deer, river otter, muskrat, raccoon, bobcat, nine-banded armadillo, Virginia opossum, and nutria, a beaver-like rodent introduced from South America for its fur.

During winter and migration, American Bitterns and Swamp Sparrows are common on Shoveler Pond, the latter located by its phoebe-like chip. The Marsh Wren is an abundant and vocal year-round resident. Check the pond's open water for wintering diving ducks such as Canvasback, Lesser Scaup, and Redhead. Although not a regular occurrence, the Masked Duck has bred here in the past—but be careful in jumping to conclusions, because Ruddy Ducks are often abundant. The generally smaller Masked Duck tends to be more secretive, avoiding open water, and is best differentiated from the Ruddy Duck by the pale line above the eye, which gives the Masked the appearance of having two dark stripes along the side of the head.

Virtually all the large wading birds recorded on the Upper Texas Coast are likely finds here, as are Fulvous

Whistling-Duck and Mottled Duck, Bufflehead in winter, and Forster's, Caspian, and Gull-billed terns. Post-breeding Wood Storks occur during summer and fall. Yellow-headed Blackbird is an uncommon migrant and well worth watching for. Orchard Oriole and Dickcissel are common breeders and vocal throughout the summer. Purple Gallinules are abundant breeders in the marshes that border the tour loop, showing up any time from mid- to late April, unlike American Coot and Common Moorhen, which remain all year.

Watch for King Rail and its broods in April, especially in the ditches bordering the rice fields and opposite Shoveler Pond. The downy black chicks lack the chestnut nape and white speckling of the locally rare Black Rail. Yellow Rails winter in the seemingly endless marshes and wet prairies of Anahuac, but seeing them requires effort and planning. Hikes into the Yellow Rail Prairie are periodically scheduled; request information at the interpretive center or contact the refuge manager at (409) 267-3337. Visitors are generally required to vacate the refuge by dusk, which precludes night viewings of Black Rail. During the warmer months, drive to the salt marsh in search of the Clapper Rail, which can be found at the very edge of the bay. Walk a few feet into the cordgrass and spend several moments scanning the water's edge.

After returning to the main entrance road, continue south toward Trinity Bay. Short-eared Owls patrol these coastal prairies in winter and spring and are best looked for around sunset. A few Sprague's Pipits winter along the road east of Crossover Road. Near the edge of the bay, watch for nesting Gull-billed Terns on open salt flats surrounded by cordgrass.

North America's only saltwater dragonfly, the extremely habitat-specific Seaside Dragonlet, can be found at the edge of the salt marshes in Anahuac. This species is small and black (males) or black and yellow (females and young males). Although its eastern mainland population ranges all the way from maritime Canada to Venezuela, it rarely strays more than a short distance inland from the muddy continental margin. These dragonflies are eaten by sparrows and shorebirds that inhabit the coastal marshes.

50: Anahuac National Wildlife Refuge, East Bay Bayou Tract

Migrations, Winter
Free, Daily
Rating: 3
FM 1985 E to East Bay Bayou Tract. Continue east 4.5 miles on FM 1985 to TX 124 to view shorebirds in the rice fields during spring migration.

TLE

American Golden-Plover

and Ruddy Turnstone. These birds constitute a guild of rice field shorebirds that associate together.

During spring, the rice fields along FM 1985 teem with shorebirds. Other species present include Mottled Duck, Fulvous Whistling-Duck, White and White-faced ibis, occasionally Glossy Ibis, and Gull-billed Tern. A late spring morning spent in this area to see the freshwater species, combined with an afternoon at Bolivar Flats to see saltwater species, will provide an excellent review of the majority of North America's regularly occurring shorebirds. By early May, young rice shoots carpet many of these fields, and most shorebirds have attained their breeding plumage. With Dickcissels rattling in the background, the sight of five hundred Hudsonian Godwits, a mass of American Golden-Plovers, or Buff-breasted Sandpipers popping their snow-white wing linings at each other while surrounded by a sea of emerald green rice sprouts will likely provide the most unforgettable experience of a birding visit to Texas.

Located roughly seven miles east from the main entrance to Anahuac NWR, the East Bayou Tract has an excellent viewshed over the rice fields and a nature trail lined with hardwoods following the bayou. Check the rice fields carefully in spring for Hudsonian Godwit, which occurs on the Upper Texas Coast precisely in this type of habitat. The species is practically unheard of on the Texas coast in fall.

Hudsonian Godwit and White-rumped Sandpiper are the last of the spring migrant shorebirds to appear. They typically arrive the third week of April and linger into May along with American Golden-Plover, Long-billed Dowitcher, Buff-breasted Sandpiper,

FINDING SEDGE AND MARSH WRENS

These birds are generally overlooked, though they can be common in the proper habitat. The Marsh Wren is often found in rushes, cattails, and other emergent vegetation—the best place at Anahuac NWR is around Shoveler Pond. In winter, look at wet marshy areas such as roadside ditches in West Harris County. The Sedge Wren prefers a drier grassy habitat and is not necessarily associated with standing water or sedge. The key to finding both of these grass wrens is to listen, then look. Marsh Wrens are vigorous, inexhaustible summer singers, continuing well into the night with their long gurgling song. Sedge Wrens also sing in the spring, with a dry, staccato, chippy delivery. The call note is their most commonly heard vocalization on the Texas coast. Dozens can easily be heard, but without some effort, not a single one will be seen. *Pisshing* is the ticket for viewing both birds. The Marsh Wren has a black saddle on the back, and the Sedge Wren is paler with finely streaked crown, wings, and mantle.

Alan Murphy, www.AlanMurphyPhotography.com

Marsh Wren

Alan Murphy, www.AlanMurphyPhotography.com

Sedge Wren

FINDING RAILS

Rails spend most of their lives in dense habitat where they are unlikely to be seen by the casual observer. They require more effort to find and are described in most books as "secretive." Finding strategies are heavy on luck and activities that plainly disturb the birds, such as dragging chains through rail habitat behind a tractor. In common with owls, nightjars, and grassland sparrows, rails are inconspicuous. In direct proportion to the difficulty involved in finding rails, they are esteemed by birders.

The saltmarsh rail species must be located by searches appropriate to the stage of the tide. This can mean searching during an especially high tide, when the water shoves the birds out of the marsh and up onto the edge of the road, or it can mean searching at low tide, when the birds are foraging in tidal channels and may come out into the open. On Yacht Basin Road (Texas Highway 83 on the Bolivar Peninsula, site 57), where Clapper Rails walk back and forth across the road before the morning traffic gets too busy, these birds can be easily seen. King Rails feed in roadside ditches along TX 124 between Winnie and High Island.

Unlike some colorful passerines that will flit out into the open to be admired at the birder's leisure, rails require us to think about the possibility of the bird's presence and scan actively for it. At Shoveler Pond on the Anahuac refuge, a careful scan along the margin of the pond and the base

RAB/Naturewide Images

King Rail

of the reeds will often turn up a Sora. The strategy for rails is to be looking for them always when in habitat. Slow movement and whispered speech are critically important in order to prevent rails from flushing.

The Clapper Rail is the predominant species and seems to occur in every salt marsh, every brackish marsh, and well inland along Galveston Bay's margins. To see a Clapper Rail, bird a tidal exchange when the water is either dropping or rising. King Rails were once far more common, but much of the freshwater marsh habitat that supported them no longer exists, making them even more difficult to locate. To find a King Rail, check suitable habitat on the Katy Prairie or rice fields, irrigation ponds, margins of interior lakes, and ditches on TX 124 between Winnie and High Island. Shoveler Pond's northern edge and the Manor Lake area in Brazoria County (site 118) can also produce a King Rail.

Clapper and King rails are poorly understood, yet they are two of the easiest rails to see. They can also be the hardest ones to identify. Attentiveness to habitat will help you find the bird, but understanding the plumage is the key to identification. There are areas of overlap and hybridization between the two, but the best field mark is the color and pattern of the mantle feathers: they are dark drab brown with gray edges on the Clapper and dark brown with buffy edges on the King. The King Rail has an overall buffy appearance and typically a richer chestnut breast with more strikingly barred flanks.

Anahuac refuge staff once provided buggy rides to view the abundant Yellow Rails that winter there. Although buggy rides have been discontinued, Yellow Rails still winter on the refuge, and patient viewing combined with muddy tennis shoes will eventually reward enthusiasts who come to add

Clapper Rail

Alan Murphy, www.AlanMurphyPhotography.com

Black Rail

Alan Murphy, www.AlanMurphyPhotography.com

this bird to a life list or who simply want to enjoy viewing the beauty of the bird. Black Rail is enigmatic. As with Yellow Rail, it is extremely difficult to locate, and once located, extremely difficult to see. For all but the most diehard birders, hearing a Black Rail is more than ample. This bird is so secretive that we know almost nothing about it. For example, we have no good estimates of local distribution or current populations. Finding a Black Rail depends first on locating it through its vocalization, which sounds something like *kicky-doo*. Mockingbirds on the coast love to sing the Black Rail's song, so beware. The Black Rail seems to prefer *Spartina spartinae,* which is a drier marsh habitat than out in the wetter smooth cordgrass. The Black Rail starts calling at dawn or dusk around the last week of February or first week of March. Moccasin Pond Trail (see site 125) is one of the best spots for lucking onto this bird. The first half mile is good, and sometimes the latter section of the trail can also be productive, varying from year to year. Once you find a territorial bird, you can hear it evening after evening; it will continue to call from the same small area.

There is no easy way to find Virginia Rails. When they are visible, it is almost exclusively at sunrise or sunset. Finding a vantage point such as a boardwalk into the marsh, and then waiting *very* quietly, is the best bet. Using a portable blind to blend in with the surrounding habitat can also work. The birds have to be comfortable before they will move out into the open.

Short of coaxing them out with a recording, the most secretive rails can be found only by zealous adherence to the strategy of listen, then look. The Sora is common in migration and not uncommon in winter. It makes a descending trill that often gives away its location down in the wet areas, underneath branches and trunks. Look hard, but expect to hear the bird before seeing it.

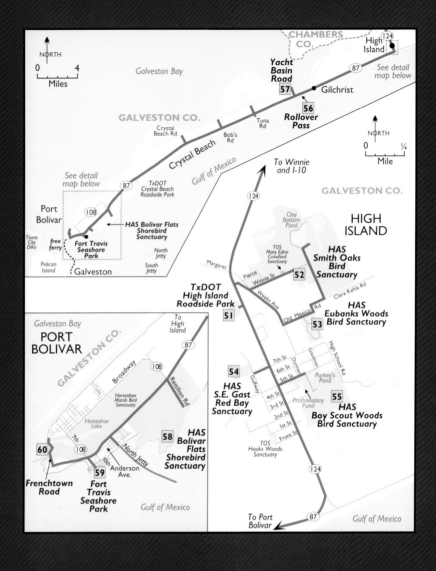

NORTH

0   4

Miles

Galveston Bay

CHAMBERS CO.

High Island 124

87   *See detail map below*

Yacht Basin Road

57

Gilchrist

56

Rollover Pass

GALVESTON CO.

Crystal Beach Rd

Tuna Rd

Bob's Rd

Crystal Beach

87

Gulf of Mexico

NORTH

0   ¼

Mile

To Winnie and I-10

124

GALVESTON CO.

See detail map below

TxDOT Crystal Beach Roadside Park

Port Bolivar

108

← *HAS Bolivar Flats Shorebird Sanctuary*

Texas City Dike

free ferry

Fort Travis Seashore Park

North Jetty

South Jetty

Pelican Island

Galveston

HIGH ISLAND

Clay Bottom Pond

TOS Mary Edna Crawford Sanctuary

HAS **Smith Oaks Bird Sanctuary**

Margaret

Pierce

Winnie St

Weeks Ave

52

Clara Kahla Rd

HAS **Eubanks Woods Bird Sanctuary**

Old Mexico Rd

53

TxDOT High Island Roadside Park

51

7th St.

6th St.

5th St.

Gulfway

Dunman

Goodman

Purkey's Pond

High School Rd

54

HAS **S.E. Gast Red Bay Sanctuary**

4th St.

3rd St.

2nd St.

1st St.

Front St.

Prothonotary Pond

55

HAS **Boy Scout Woods Bird Sanctuary**

TOS Hooks Woods Sanctuary

124

87

To Port Bolivar

Gulf of Mexico

Galveston Bay

PORT BOLIVAR

GALVESTON CO.

To High Island

87

108

Broadway

Rettilion Rd

Horseshoe Marsh Bird Sanctuary

Horseshoe Lake

7th

108

North Jetty

58

HAS **Bolivar Flats Shorebird Sanctuary**

60

Frenchtown Road

10th

Anderson Ave.

59

Fort Travis Seashore Park

Gulf of Mexico

Bolivar Loop

The linear extent of the sites on the Bolivar Loop is not much more than twenty-five miles, but this loop contains both High Island and Bolivar Flats, two of the best known birding sites in Texas. The aggregate bird list for these two sites is greater than that of many multistate regions in the United States and constitutes the highest profile spring birding venue in the nation. Most of the sites lie along the Bolivar Peninsula, a narrow finger of land that defines the southern margin of the eastern portion of Galveston Bay. Opposite the tip of the peninsula is the eastern end of Galveston Island, the location of the next loop. Between the end of the peninsula and Galveston Island is the Houston Ship Channel, the shipping lane that made Houston a great inland port.

Before beach houses, gas stations, and restaurants dotted the Bolivar Peninsula, the original inhabitants of what was later to become known as the Upper Texas Coast were Karankawa Indians, warriors who hunted with bows and traveled in canoes. Their contacts with European explorers varied from hostile to friendly. Like many modern Texans, the Karankawa fished and gathered shellfish in the bays along the coast and hunted game inland. They lived in bands, periodically gathering in large groups. Unfortunately, the Karankawa were gone by 1850 and, other than a few descriptions of their language and logs indicating their travels with early explorers, little is known about them.

Today oil wells and herds of cattle are prominent sights along the peninsula, shrimpers from Port Bolivar ply the Gulf and bay waters, and new service providers cater to the tourist trade with car washes, tanning parlors, pizza joints, and several motels. All of this development hinges on the belief that no hurricane will ever again erase all human-made structures from the surface of the peninsula. If a storm ever does so, the peninsula will once again be a place the Karankawa would recognize as their home.

Birding on the Bolivar Loop is defined by the Gulf of Mexico, Galveston Bay, the tides, and the few trees

RAB/Naturewide Images

Bolivar Flats

planted by settlers. Most sites on the loop are no more than a couple of feet above sea level, and many are periodically submerged. Other than the various wooded sanctuaries at High Island, most of this loop's sites host a great diversity of waterbirds; indeed, this is one of the finest places in the country to observe a large diversity of sandpipers, plovers, terns, and large waders. Because of the rich assemblage of waterbirds, it is virtually impossible to have a bad day of birding at these sites at any time of the year. Spring and fall migration present an additional host of land bird species, making the birding here an unforgettable experience.

Most birders who make their first pilgrimage to Texas for spring migration begin at High Island. This venue has gone from an unknown spoil-filled blip on the map, where in the early 1970s spring migration netted barely ten birders even on a weekend after a fallout, to a major tourism destination that can be uncomfortably crowded on peak days. Those who assemble to watch the avian parade are accommodated by bleachers, boardwalks, and other modern conveniences unknown to High Island birders a few scant decades ago. The seasonal tourism crunch puts a premium on lodging—plan your trip well in advance or expect to stay in accommodations that are well-removed from High Island itself. Houston,

Beaumont, and Galveston all constitute overflow sites for High Island during spring weekends.

The dynamic, ever-changing nature of spring migration at High Island does not mean that visits should be randomly timed. The ideal spring visit to High Island occurs immediately after the passage of a cold front or late-season storm. The combined effects of wind, rain, and cold on migrating passerines causes them to make landfall at the first possible place. Large-scale groundings of migrants, however hard these are on the birds themselves, provide an unforgettable experience for the birder. Follow weather conditions on the Internet or the Weather Channel and recognize that the itinerary should be dictated by the weather. Pay careful attention to the regular postings on TexBirds, the listserve dedicated to general reporting of bird activity in the state. Most important, in the mad rush to reach High Island, take time to stop and check out each and every stand of trees for potential finds. During spring migration, the best treasures will often be found in relatively unbirded sites.

Clear days with a prevailing southeast wind will result in relatively low numbers of migrants, because the birds take advantage of the tailwind and push on toward their more northerly destinations. Particularly on these days visitors should make sure to tour a diversity of sites reflecting varied habitat—Anahuac, its surrounding rice fields, sites on the Sabine Loop, and Bolivar Flats are all venues that can produce exceptional spring migration days. "Southerly" days are also good times to look for migrant hawks and to check grassy areas for migrating sparrows. Again, the key for birders anticipating a big day is to hit a diversity of sites with the maximal diversity of habitats.

Birders on the coast whose visits do not coincide with northerly weather systems should focus their passerine birding on sites farther inland. Big Thicket venues will be filling up with the neotropical migrants that have come to the woodland areas of East Texas to nest, and numerous warbler and vireo species can be expected.

First-time visitors and beginning birders may want to start their High Island visit at Boy Scout Woods (site 55). This site is staffed during spring and is an excellent place to obtain information about the most recent sightings.

51: TxDOT High Island Roadside Park

Migrations
Free, Daily
Rating: 1
From I-10 in Winnie, TX 124 S to High Island. Stop at TxDOT High Island

TLE

Spicebush Swallowtail

Roadside Park for maps and
information.

The first documented Connecticut
Warbler in Texas appeared in the oaks
around the picnic tables, but virtually
any spring or fall migrant songbird
is possible. During late spring, the
grassy area to the south may host a
few Bobolinks.

52: Houston Audubon Society Smith Oaks Bird Sanctuary

Migrations
Site fee, Daily
Rating: 3
From the TxDOT High Island Road-
side Park, TX 124 N 0.2 mile; Weeks
Avenue S 0.1 mile; Winnie Street E
0.2 mile to Smith Oaks Bird Sanc-
tuary.

High Island visitors need to purchase
an annual season patch or a day pass

before entering the various sanctuaries. Both are on sale at Smith Oaks throughout spring as well as at Boy Scout Woods and at the Edith L. Moore Nature Sanctuary in Houston (site 94). Several of the magnificent live oaks now exceed one hundred years in age. During spring migration throngs of vireos, warblers, tanagers, orioles, and buntings land in these trees after completing their nonstop flights across the Gulf of Mexico. Smith Oaks contains the most extensive woodland of the High Island sanctuaries; plan to spend considerable time here and at adjacent sites. Although few birders go to Smith Oaks hunting for rarities, birds such as Black-throated Gray Warbler, West-

ern Tanager, Black-headed Grosbeak, Black-whiskered Vireo, and Yellow-green Vireo have been observed in recent years.

Portions of the woods have boardwalks. They provide wheelchair access and protect the undergrowth but can be slippery after a rain. Rubber-soled, mid-calf footgear allows exploration of some of the less popular trails in comfort and helps fend off the poison ivy that makes up much of the understory. Bring insect repellent.

Houston Audubon Society Smith Oaks Bird Sanctuary

RAB/Naturewide Images

Rufous Hummingbird

RAB/Naturewide Images

53: Houston Audubon Society Eubanks Woods Bird Sanctuary, Hummingbird and Butterfly Garden, and Claybottom Pond

Migrations
Site fee, Daily
Rating: 2
From TxDOT High Island Roadside Park, travel north on TX 124 0.2 mile; Weeks Avenue S 0.4 miles; Old Mexico Road E 0.1 mile to Eubanks Woods Bird Sanctuary.

During wet weather the boardwalk at this Houston Audubon Society sanctuary provides dry access to part of the woods. The shaded pond within the woods is worth checking for waterthrushes and Prothonotary Warbler. Dragonflies such as the Eastern Pondhawk and the less common Great Pondhawk may be numerous at the sunny entrance to the woods, often feeding on smaller insects disturbed by foot traffic.

Continuing east on Old Mexico Road you will reach the eastern entrance to Smith Oaks Bird Sanctuary; watch for a small sign indicating a left turn. During certain times of the year this gate is locked, necessitating entrance via the Winnie Street entrance. At the end of the entrance road is a parking lot. Across the fence that borders the parking lot is a hummingbird and butterfly garden. Watch for showy species of butterflies including Gulf Fritillary, Giant Swallowtail, Cloudless Sulphur, Monarch, Pearl Crescent, and various skippers. Portable toilets are available during spring migration.

Although Ruby-throated Hummingbirds occur frequently, Rufous, Black-chinned, and with great luck wintering Broad-tailed hummingbirds may linger into spring. Behind the garden, note Purple Martin houses and a freshwater reservoir. Both species of cormorants, Anhinga, Pied-billed Grebe, or a few swallows may be present, plus turtles, frogs, and dragonflies such as Eastern Amberwing and Roseate Skimmer. The trail separating the reservoir from the

Giant Swallowtail

RAB./Naturewide Images

back of Smith Oaks can be very birdy and affords good visibility of the forest edge. Please remember to close all gates.

Across the fence from the parking lot is a red brick building, a reminder of High Island's petroleum shipping days. From this building a trail leads through large moss-draped live oaks that are part of the Smith Oaks Sanctuary and are often full of birds. Follow this trail several hundred feet to wooden stairs ascending a dike. This dike borders Claybottom Pond on the north side of Smith Oaks, also owned and protected by Houston Audubon Society. Nearby on the left is an island with a mixed heronry with nesting Neotropic Cormorants and at least

eight species of large waders, including Roseate Spoonbill, Snowy Egret, Little Blue and Tricolored herons, and Black-crowned Night-Heron. Prior to the Audubon Society's involvement, human disturbance prevented this nesting colony from developing. The island became part of the sanctuary, and in 1996 birds began to nest there, using it as a night roost as well outside the nesting season. This island is quite close to the dike, so speak in whispers and do not hesitate to shush anyone who does not understand how easily nesting birds can be disturbed. This site provides a rare opportunity to watch and listen as the birds display, build nests, breed, fight, and rear their young. In the after-

Houston Audubon Society S. E. Gast Red Bay Sanctuary

noon, great flights of herons, egrets, and ibis that have been foraging in the nearby marshes return to roost on the island. Close access to the island may not be available during March or early April while nests are being established, but even so, birds should be at reasonable binocular or telescope distance. The Claybottom Pond rookery was severely damaged by Hurricane Rita. Both dead and live nesting trees, primarily cypress and willow, were lost or damaged. Both tree planting and artificial platforms are being employed as a means of mitigating the losses. Portions of the rookery remain and provide nesting habitat. Viewing remains excellent.

54: Houston Audubon Society S. E. Gast Red Bay Sanctuary

Migrations
Site fee, Daily
Rating: 1
From TxDOT Roadside Park, TX 124 S 0.4 mile; 7th Street W 0.1 mile to sanctuary.

The S. E. Gast Red Bay Sanctuary sits on the western edge of High Island, offering woodland birding as well as a view of the coastal prairie that surrounds the salt dome. Check the pond at the entrance for migrants. During winter, expect White-throated and Song sparrows, American Robin,

Brown Thrasher, kinglets, Yellow-rumped Warbler, and Northern Cardinal; lingering warblers or a Gray Catbird are possible. Check the sanctuary's scrubby margins for Sedge Wren and Le Conte's Sparrow.

This sanctuary, like some others on the trail, provides benches that allow birders to take advantage of the dynamic nature of migration. The scope and pace of change during migration is such that rather than chasing the birds, birders can often see just as many species at a given venue by simply sitting down and watching the procession of birds moving through the trees.

55: Houston Audubon Society Boy Scout Woods Bird Sanctuary

Migrations
Site fee, Daily
Rating: 3
From TxDOT Roadside Park, TX 124 S 0.5 mile; 5th Street E 0.2 mile to Boy Scout Woods Bird Sanctuary. Parking lot on right, and limited street parking along south side of road only. Do not make U-turns in driveways.

Throughout spring, Houston Audubon Society operates an information booth and gift shop in the sanctuary. Annual and day passes may be purchased here. Check the garden just inside the gate and on the right for hummingbirds and butterflies.

RAB./Naturewide Images

Orchard Oriole

RAB/Naturewide Images

Indigo Bunting

Purkey's Pond, in front of the viewing stands, often attracts Prothonotary Warbler, waterthrushes, and Green Heron, but many other species also come in to bathe. During summer and early fall dragonflies such as Great Blue Skimmer, Great Pondhawk, and Roseate Skimmer are common here.

One sanctuary path goes into the garden. Ringed by red mulberry trees, it can be alive with Gray Catbirds, warblers, tanagers, buntings, and grosbeaks. Watch out for fire ant mounds underfoot; standing in one can be extremely painful. Continue along the boardwalk, veering left into the woods and the Cathedral area, once a narrow woodland trail but recently opened up by hurricane damage. Bear to the left, go outside the woods again to Bessie's Pond, and bird back to the entrance gate. Remember that the diversity of birds within the sanctuary can change by the minute, so do not hesitate to retrace and backtrack numerous times.

Return to the Cathedral area. From here, dirt trails lead into and out of the woods. Watch for a turnstile leading to the field south of the woods, where an elevated walkway skirts a small pond. During spring Sedge Wren, Orchard Oriole, Blue Grosbeak, and both Painted and Indigo buntings may be scattered through the weedy growth and small clumps of trees. Other trails lead into viney tangles where Hooded, Worm-eating, Kentucky, and Swainson's warblers lurk.

Take some time to review the sightings board at the information booth. Cast an eye upward for the Chimney Swifts and Purple Martins that hunt over the woods and gardens, occasionally joined by various swallows. Broad-winged, Sharp-shinned, and Cooper's hawks, Merlins, Peregrine Falcons, Mississippi Kites, and the occasional Swallow-tailed Kite also pass over these woods.

Labor Day weekends here and in other woods and thickets along the coast provide a wealth of *Empidonax* flycatchers. Fall migration, although less intense than that of spring, is an excellent time to bird High Island. The crowds are sparse or nonexistent, and the birding can be exceptional. In late fall, try birding the coast during the passage of the first cold fronts. Fifteen or twenty species of warblers can occur here, plus a variety of vireos, flycatchers, and other birds. Early cold fronts also produce striking movements of butterflies, including Monarch, Common Buckeye, and Ocola Skipper, species that breed northward during summer then migrate south in the fall.

From 5th Street, continue 0.9 mile south on Texas Highway 124 to TX 87, located just inland from the Gulf dunes. Just before reaching the grassy triangle that divides the traffic lanes, turn left through a swinging pipe gate (occasionally locked). This rough road goes into the south High Island oil field. Once on the dirt road, left turns are generally prohibited. Proceed carefully on the dirt road for 0.4 mile. A large, shallow depression between the dirt road and the Gulf holds a lake during all but the driest months. Depending on the water level, ducks, the usual large wading birds—including Little Blue and Tricolored herons, various ibis, and Roseate Spoonbills—shorebirds, gulls, terns, and other species come here to feed, bathe, and loaf in the shallows. Long-tailed Duck and Black-legged Kittiwake have been recorded here; Yellow-headed Blackbirds and Black Tern are often seen during spring migration. In spring or summer watch for nesting Black-necked Stilt, Killdeer, Wilson's Plover, Willet, Common Nighthawk, and Eastern Meadowlark as well as the locally rare Marl Pennant, a black dragonfly with just a slender band of black at the base of the hind wing. Other dragonflies at the lake include Black, Carolina, and Red saddlebags as well as other large skimmers. Photographers take note: many excellent waterbird photos have been taken at this site by people shooting from their car windows.

This road continues to the north side of town just south of the bridge over the Gulf Intracoastal Waterway.

The gate at the far end of the road that provides an exit to TX 124 may not be open, requiring a U-turn.

The beach road, TX 87, may still be driven a short distance east of High Island. Watch for flocks of terns and unusual gulls such as Thayer's and Glaucous. During migration, check even the smallest salt cedars for migrants. Most of TX 87 is washed out between High Island and Port Arthur and should not be attempted even in a four-wheel-drive vehicle. Besides the near certainty of getting stuck in the soft sand, the presence of buried lengths of barbed wire and thousands of large catfish spines pose a significant threat of punctures along this stretch of the beach.

56: Rollover Pass

All Seasons
Free, Daily
Rating: 3
From intersection of TX 124 and TX 87, take TX 87 S 7.2 miles to Rollover Pass.

Rollover Pass is an artificial cut across the Bolivar Peninsula where Forster's Terns join Texas anglers to pursue fish moving between the Gulf and East Bay. The tidal cut has formed an extensive sediment flat on the bay side of the peninsula, where at low tide thousands of feeding and roosting shorebirds can be seen, along with gulls, terns, herons, and pelicans. Watch for Reddish Egret, American Avocet, and American Oystercatcher. Marbled Godwits are present during most months of the year. Colonial waterbird rookeries on spoil islands in the bay include nesting Roseate Spoonbills. Most birders scan the rich flats, islands, and sand bars on the bay side of the road, and then move on. However, birds absent from the bay side of the cut may occur in the nearshore waters just across the road, including scaup, mergansers, a few scoters, and hundreds of Bonaparte's Gulls as well as rarities such as Long-tailed Duck and Long-tailed Jaeger.

Take a few minutes to work the Gulf side of the cut and do not ignore the birds roosting on the pilings; Black-legged Kittiwake has been seen here. During rising tides the bay side of Rollover Pass can be an excellent spot for bird photographers, and terns flying beats through the cut provide a great subject for flight photos. A scope is suggested for this site. Generally, high tides are best as the birds are closer to the parking lot. This is an excellent spot to work on gull and tern identification; frequently other birders are present and available to help with a vexing identification problem.

Roseate Spoonbills

57: Yacht Basin Road

All Seasons
Free, Daily
Rating: 1
Just half a mile southwest of Rollover Pass (site 56), turn north on Yacht Basin Road. A narrow two-lane road passes through salt marsh and dead-ends at a boat launch along the Gulf Intracoastal Waterway.

This is an excellent site to scan for a variety of waterbirds (perhaps the most famous of which was a Black Noddy that occurred here during

RAB/Naturewide Images

Gull-billed Tern

April of 1998); watch for jaegers amid the hordes of Laughing Gulls that follow the shrimp boats into port. Clapper Rail, Willet, and Seaside Sparrow nest in the cordgrass marsh, and the sand flats often host Wilson's Plover, Whimbrel, and a variety of gulls and terns, including Gull-billed Tern. During winter and spring, watch for Nelson's Sharp-tailed Sparrow alongside the Seaside Sparrows, especially in tidally inundated salt marsh closest to the end of the road. Hearing and seeing both of these sparrows side by side is often an unexpected bonus for attentive birders working the coast during April. Please do not enter the lawns or driveways of private residences at the end of the road.

Continuing southwest toward Bolivar Flats, there are several roads that lead to the Intracoastal Waterway. Infrequently, a Black Rail is observed in these marshes; Clapper Rail is regular and reasonably easy to see. Among these roads are Tuna Drive (4.1 miles from Yacht Basin); Bob Road (3.8 miles from Tuna), where Curlew Sandpiper and Ruff have occurred; and Crystal Beach Road (0.7 mile from Bob Road). Wherever large numbers of gulls are bathing or loafing in the shallows along these roads, check for Franklin's Gull, Black-legged Kittiwake, and other locally uncommon species. Remember: the land bordering these roads is private—bird from the roadside only.

Another 4.6 miles past Crystal Beach Road, watch for the Crystal Beach TxDOT Roadside Park. Watch for Gregory Park on the Gulf side of the road, where the crab festival is held in June. During migration this field, with a picnic pavilion in its center, often hosts Yellow-headed Blackbird and, less frequently, Bobolink. A few songbirds use the tall shrubs at the Gulf side of the field near the livestock pens; Clay-colored Sparrow has occurred in spring.

58: Houston Audubon Society Bolivar Flats Shorebird Sanctuary

All Seasons
Free, Daily
Rating: 3
From TxDOT Park in Crystal Beach, TX 87 S 2.6 miles; Loop 108/Rettilon Road S 0.4 mile to beach. Follow tire tracks W on hard-packed sand to vehicular barrier posts bordering the Bolivar Flats Shorebird Sanctuary. Do not drive beyond the posts.

Bolivar Flats is one of the best spots on the Gulf of Mexico to study a variety of waterbirds. Tens of thousands of gulls, terns, shorebirds, and herons feed on the flats, and huge flocks that include American White Pelican and Brown Pelican roost here during high tide.

RAB/Naturewide Images

American Avocets

American Avocets winter on the flats, as do more than a hundred endangered Piping Plovers as well as numerous Snowy and Semipalmated plovers. The flats are a staging area for northbound avocets, and the sight of up to ten thousand of these birds in their red, black, and white breeding plumage massed on the flats just prior to continuing northward is one of the most memorable sights a birder can have in this part of Texas. Wilson's Plover, Willet, Black-necked Stilt, White-tailed Kite, Horned Lark, and Seaside Sparrow nest at Bolivar. Nelson's Sharp-tailed Sparrows winter in the tidally inundated cordgrass, and Peregrine Falcons and Merlin frequently dive-bomb the shorebird flocks. Photographic opportunities abound—this site is a must. During nesting season, walk along the water's edge whenever possible to avoid flushing Least Terns from their nests and to avoid stepping on eggs or young birds.

From Rettilon Road, continue southwest 1.9 miles on Texas Highway 87 to the North Jetty. At low tide, a walk down the jetty will provide good views of the feeding birds dispersed across Bolivar Flats.

59: Fort Travis Seashore Park

Migrations
Free, Daily
Rating: 1
From site 58, TX 87 S 0.5 mile to sign for Gulf and to Fort Travis Seashore Park.

During spring, check mowed lawns within the park for American Golden-Plover and Black-bellied Plover, Upland and Buff-breasted sandpipers, pipits, Bobolinks, and other grass-loving species. During migration, scrutinize the scrubby thickets surrounding

Groove-billed Ani

TLE

Reddish Egret

FINDING REDDISH EGRETS

Of all the locally nesting herons and egrets, this is the most faithfully coastal, rarely seen any distance inland. Some young birds wander but rarely away from the immediate coast. The white morph of the Reddish Egret is often overlooked because it resembles Snowy and Great egrets. Find this bird by looking for its exaggerated, staggering, drunken-looking movements. In summer look for an intensely pink dark-tipped bill on both color forms. East Beach on Galveston Island and Bolivar Flats (site 58) are good sites for Reddish Egret. White morph birds and the occasional dark bird with some white plumage are most often seen along the bay side of west Galveston Island.

RAB/Naturewide Images

Reddish Egret (white morph)

American Oystercatchers

the park for the occasional Groove-billed Ani as well as Blue Grosbeak, Indigo and Painted buntings, Yellow Warbler, Nashville Warbler, and the locally uncommon Cape May Warbler. During weekends or holidays, this site may be too crowded to bird effectively.

60: Frenchtown Road

All Seasons
Free, Daily
Rating: 2
From site 59, continue on TX 87 S 1.1 miles; Frenchtown Road N toward Port Bolivar.

The beach and oyster-covered flats that flank the road attract a variety of species. American Oystercatcher is often present during low tide, as is Clapper Rail, and any number of shorebirds, ducks, or large waders may occur. Photographers may also obtain marsh shots that include the Bolivar Lighthouse and sunset images with silhouettes of the masts of the fishing boats moored at Port Bolivar.

From Frenchtown Road, continue southwest 0.2 miles on Texas Highway 87 to the tip of the Bolivar Peninsula and the Bolivar ferry landing. During weekends, holidays, or special events, there can be long ferry waits. Otherwise the wait is typically brief, as several boats shuttle back and forth across the channel. Once aboard the ferry but before it leaves the dock, go to the side of the ship and observe or photograph the Laughing Gulls, Neotropic Cormorants (mostly in summer), and Double-crested Cormorants that roost on the pilings just a few feet away. The ferry crosses the ship channel that leads to the port of Houston.

Scan for ferry rarities such as Black-legged Kittiwake (winter) and Sooty Tern (spring). During summer, Magnificent Frigatebird may be seen.

The ferry crossing is free and takes about 15–20 minutes, depending on traffic. During the crossing, go to the stern, where Laughing Gulls and several species of terns may be photographed at close range. The gulls often snatch food from upraised fingers, occasionally mistaking the fingers for food. Be aware that this is one of the most predictable sites in Texas to have clothing decorated by Laughing Gulls, so wear a wide-brimmed hat and look directly upward as little as possible. Bathrooms are located on the second deck. Bottlenose dolphins are frequently seen, especially off Sea Wolf Park, and on rare occasions approach the ferry to ride the bow wave.

Spoil islands that were created by the dredging required to make the ship channel are visible from the deck of the ferry and are home to vast breeding colonies of Laughing Gulls.

FINDING GRASSLAND SPARROWS

The taxonomic classification of "Little Brown Jobber" may not have received official acceptance, but finding and identifying these cryptic birds constitutes one of the chief joys of birding—or one of its chief frustrations. The challenge for any grassland bird is to avoid detection. Secretive, silent, and drab, these birds have developed a survival strategy that revolves around blending in. Even in spring they are openly seen only at the hormone-crazed peak of breeding season, and then only with vocalizations that mimic insect songs to mislead predators. They are practically invisible to the keenest-eyed predators of the plains and consequently all but invisible to you. Birders listening for vocalizations encounter these spirits of the grass only with some difficulty.

Birders who have some familiarity with and curiosity about sparrows most often have in mind larger, boldly marked birds such as Savannah, White-crowned, or White-throated sparrows—birds that sit on perches

Seacoast Bluestem

and provide accommodating views. The grassland sparrows are not bold in either appearance or behavior. Hence the only way to find these birds after identifying the correct habitat is to entice them into the open. *Pisshing* is the ideal way to do this.

Texas is sparrow-rich, and targets such as Le Conte's, Grasshopper, Henslow's, and Nelson's Sharp-tailed sparrows are all found first and foremost by identifying proper habitat, within which they are nondescript, nonvocal, and inconspicuous.

Understand the grassland mosaic that these birds prefer in the winter, and the effort will be richly repaid. They prefer different types of grass communities and can be extremely specific in their choice of wintering sites. Le Conte's Sparrow is expected both coastally and inland in prairie with low, scattered shrubs (see p. 193). Moist prairie pockets may be more productive. Grasshopper Sparrow is more likely inland in drier prairie (see p. 191). Henslow's may be in shrubby prairie or grassy forest understory (see p. 36). Nelson's Sharp-tailed Sparrow occurs, as we have mentioned, in inundated salt marsh (see p. 60).

Along the Texas coast, wintering Le Conte's Sparrow and Nelson's Sharp-tailed Sparrow exhibit orange breasts and dark cheek patches. Additionally, Le Conte's shares the sharp-tailed sparrow's orange supercilium and largely unstreaked breast. Field marks and range render separation of adults a fairly simple matter. Le Conte's differs from Nelson's Sharp-tailed Sparrow by possessing a white rather than gray crown stripe, and it has a streaked hindneck. Le Conte's Sparrow is widespread but localized and typically occurs farther inland.

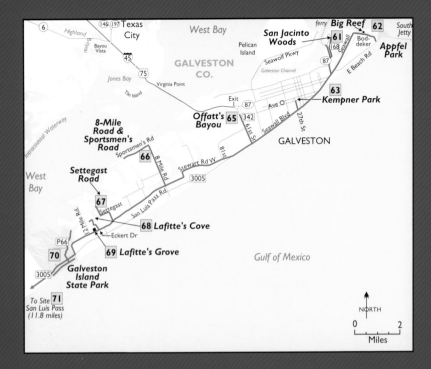

Galveston Loop

Galveston, once the largest city in Texas, occupies the eastern end of a long, slender barrier island. It is separated from the mainland by a narrow arm of Galveston Bay that varies from about two to four miles in width. The island may be reached by bridge or ferry at its east end or by bridge at the west end. When the Karankawa Indians roamed Galveston Island, the habitat was a simple mosaic of coastal prairie and marsh grasses, prickly pear cactus, and a few shrubs. A small grove of trees near the island's west end, Lafitte's Grove, may have occurred naturally, but the island was essentially treeless. Beginning in 1528, the island experienced a long history of European visitation and settlement that included Spanish explorers and surveyors and the French pirate Jean Lafitte. Since that time the island's habitats have been modified by ditching, draining, grazing, housing tracts, urban development, channel dredging, the construction of jetties, a seawall, and the planting of innumerable lawns and thousands of trees.

With thirty-two miles of beach and countless acres of mudflats and tidal sloughs, birding is good in Galveston throughout the year. John James Audubon visited Galveston Bay and wrote glowingly about the numerous waterbirds. Ever since, birders and naturalists have been thrilled by the sight of shorebird-packed mudflats, tidal channels jammed with ibis and Roseate Spoonbills, and sand flats covered with nesting terns and Black Skimmers. The larger waders are ever present, and except for a few weeks during June and early July, shorebirds are abundant.

During summer Galveston is hot and muggy, with the added excitement of possible hurricanes. Breeding Least Terns and Black Skimmers are common in summer, hundreds to thousands of nonbreeding Black Terns spend the summer at San Luis Pass, Wilson's Plovers chase fiddler crabs through the salt marshes, and (rarely) a Black Rail may be heard on the west end of the island. During winter the weather is generally still warm and muggy, but a stiff north breeze can make the town feel like Chicago in November. Check the

seawall's endless Gulf vista for shorebirds, gulls, terns, and Northern Gannet. It was along this road that British
birders discovered the state's first
Wandering Tattler.

Superb venues on this loop include
Big Reef Park on East Beach, Galveston Island State Park, and San Luis
Pass on the western end of the island.
Galveston's attractions for the traveling birder are manifold. Its variety
of habitats conducive to landbirds,
waterbirds, and shorebirds, the regular sightings of rare or unusual species, generally mild weather, access
to quality lodging and good food, and
proximity to Houston all combine to
make Galveston and its affiliated sites
one of the best loops on the Great
Texas Coastal Birding Trail.

Yellow-rumped (Myrtle) Warbler

61: San Jacinto Woods (Previously the Corps Woods at Galveston)

Migrations
Free, Daily
Rating: 1
From the Bolivar ferry, TX 87 S 0.6
mile; TX 168 N 0.6 mile to San
Jacinto Woods; parking area on
the right.

This narrow woodlot, composed of
a variety of native and introduced
species, has been improved as a birding destination with funds from the
Great Texas Coastal Birding Trail.

The trail is lined with cactus and a
variety of wildflowers and leads to
two short boardwalks, each ending in
a deck over a channel that parallels
the margin of the woods. Approaching the channel, watch for teal,
Gadwall, other puddle ducks, Belted
Kingfisher, and turtles. Green Heron
and Black-crowned Night-Heron are
often present. During spring, Indigo
Buntings and a few Painted Buntings
may congregate here, but a light rain
or cold front can pack the trees with
warblers and other migrants. Expect
less activity during winter, but species
to look for include Brown Thrasher,
White-throated Sparrow, Blue-gray

Gnatcatcher, and the ubiquitous Yellow-rumped Warbler. During the warmer months peer downward from the decks and scan the channel's margins for small, slender dragonflies that become quite common. The black males and black and yellow females belong to the aforementioned Seaside Dragonlet, our only true saltwater dragonfly in North America.

62: Big Reef and Appfel Park

All Seasons
Site fee, Daily
Rating: 3
From site 61, return to TX 87 S 0.7 mile; Seawall Blvd. N 2.0 miles to

dead end. Scan across the channel toward the Bolivar Flats. Turn right (east) to reach Big Reef platform and boardwalk after 0.3 mile.

Big Reef, an extensive dune and marsh community isolated by the entrance to Galveston Bay, may be reached by crossing a small bridge located adjacent to an elevated platform on the east side of the entrance road. Thousands of shorebirds, gulls, Black Skimmers, and terns roost on this sand spit. Look for more unusual gulls such as Great and Lesser Black-backed, Thayer's, Glaucous, and Franklin's. Both of the local kinds of cormorants and Red-breasted Merganser feed in the channel between

RAB/Naturewide Images

Black Skimmers

the road and the dunes. There are usually a few Reddish Egrets around; these clever birds have learned to steal small fish from anglers' bait buckets. Plovers and sandpipers feed in the channel. They and other species are often close enough to photograph successfully. The first Kelp Gull in Texas appeared at this location, so obviously anything can turn up—and does: Elegant Tern occurred here in the fall of 2001, spotted by David Sibley during a field trip that had been coordinated with a book-signing event in Galveston.

Continue south on the entrance road to Appfel Park, one of the most popular recreational beaches in Texas. During spring, summer, and fall there is an entry fee for this part of the beach. If it is crowded with sunbathers, the birding here is negligible. Look for jaegers and Northern Gannets working the waters around the South Jetty. This is an excellent area to study and photograph gulls and terns, including Sandwich Tern. Photographers will get best results by using their vehicle as a blind. During winter, watch for Piping Plover, Glaucous Gull, and Merlin. California Gull and other rarities have occurred here in spring. On winter days the beach can be virtually deserted, with the exception of a few anglers. Avoid soft sand and deep tidal channels, and if a mist rolls in, follow the vehicle tracks back to the road. Also, do not drive beyond the barriers that separate this beach from the Big Reef dunes.

63: Kempner Park

Migrations
Free, Daily
Rating: 2
From Seawall Blvd.; 27th St. N 0.4 mile; park is at Avenue O.

When spring weather conditions are favorable, migrant landbirds swarm the oaks in and around this park and the adjacent mansion, especially the interlaced live oak branches just behind the fence on the western margin of the park. The American

Hooded Warbler

FINDING NEOTROPIC CORMORANTS

Previously, small numbers of this common breeding bird were found in winter only along the immediate coast. In recent years it has become a common wintering bird on ponds and bayous in the Houston vicinity as well. Look at cormorants perched on pilings at East Beach on Galveston Island. Find the Neotropic Cormorant by searching for a cormorant that is significantly smaller than the Double-crested. In mixed flocks look for smaller birds with more rapid wingbeats. Young birds typically lack the extensive white underparts of the Double-crested Cormorant. On perched birds, notice that the lores of adult Neotropic Cormorants are feathered, whereas they are naked and orange on Double-crested Cormorants. Additionally, Neotropic lacks the large, orange gular (or throat) patch characteristic of the Double-crested.

Neotropic Cormorant

Robin, which is locally uncommon, occasionally nests here. Also check the neighborhood for White-winged Dove, a commonly occurring bird. In spring, scan the fruiting mulberry trees in this area for orioles, tanagers, grosbeaks, and other "mulberry birds" that often occur in large numbers. The often densely planted edges of the mansion grounds attract Kentucky, Hooded, Worm-eating, and Swainson's warblers. Other terrestrial birds occur here as well, but access to the interior grounds is not allowed. During warmer winters the park and surrounding neighborhoods attract lingering warblers and are worth checking.

64: Site removed from trail

65: Offatt's Bayou

Migrations, Winter
Free, Daily
Rating: 1
From Broadway W; 61st Street/Spur 342 S 0.3 mile to bayou. View from two boat ramp parking areas on the west side of 61st Street.

Offatt's Bayou is quite deep, and the water is unusually clear, providing good fishing conditions for the loons, grebes, and diving ducks that are often abundant during winter and late spring. Dozens of Common Loons

are often present. These large northern waterbirds may be encountered at other local sites such as the Texas City Dike (site 74) but are most easily observed at Offatt's Bayou, where they often feed a few feet from shore. Viewing is best in late April when, just prior to returning north, they have assumed their checkered black and white breeding plumage. Other common species on the bayou include: Eared and other grebes, scaup and various diving ducks, and Red-breasted Merganser. During migration and winter, Bonaparte's Gulls are often present by the hundreds. Offatt's Bayou may also be viewed from other areas along its margin, including the parking lot of Moody Gardens. During good loon winters it is worth exploring a bit to look for Pacific (rare) and Red-throated (very rare) loons, both of which have occurred here.

66: 8-Mile Road and Sportsmen's Road

All Seasons
Free, Daily
Rating: 2
On Stewart Road W, cross 81st Street, continue 2.9 miles; 8-Mile Road N 1.7 miles to West Galveston Bay and Sportsmen's Road.

The north-south roads that cross Galveston Island have birdlife all year

Common Loon

FINDING LOONS

The deep, clear waters of Offatt's Bayou (site 65) attract the most significant populations of loons on the Upper Texas Coast. Loons require clear water to hunt their fish, hence their distribution is determined by water clarity. The Common Loon is indeed the most common species, yet in most years at least one Pacific Loon can be found in late winter and early spring associating with Common Loon flocks. Red-throated Loon is the least common of the three but has been found in waters along the Texas City Dike (site 74), Offatt's Bayou, and the base of Quintana Jetty (site 122).

Loon finding demands a good scope and patience. Find a vantage point and work slowly through the flocks of loons as they dive, remain submerged for some minutes, and pop up to the surface for a few moments. After watching a few hundred Common Loons for a few hundred hours, identification becomes easy! The Common Loon is variable, and small ones are shaped much like Pacific Loon. In West Galveston Bay, another excellent place to watch for these birds, it is not unusual to hear the call of a Common Loon.

TLE

Whimbrel

but are most interesting during spring when they attract hundreds to thousands of American Golden-Plovers and smaller numbers of Whimbrels, Long-billed Curlews, and Upland, Buff-breasted, and Baird's sandpipers. Watch also for White-tailed Kite, Northern Harrier, Loggerhead Shrike, and wintering Sandhill Cranes. Check the north end of 8-Mile Road, scanning the rubble- and shell-covered shore for American Oystercatcher, and scan the bay for Common Goldeneye, Magnificent Frigatebird, and other waterbirds. Go west on Sportsmen's Road and bird its margins until it ends. Be careful not to impede traffic. The marshes along Sportsmen's Road come right to the edge of the pavement, and species such as White Ibis, Roseate Spoonbill, Tricolored Heron, Snowy Egret, and Clapper Rail may be very close, offering excellent photographic opportunities. Seaside Sparrows nest here, and Nelson's Sharp-tailed Sparrows occur during winter. At the end of Sportsmen's Road the rubble spit and muddy flats

FINDING MOTTLED DUCKS

Although waterfowl are a significant part of the winter bird population on the Upper Texas Coast, only a few species breed here. Both species of whistling-ducks, Blue-winged Teal, Wood Duck, and Mottled Duck are the expected nesters. The Mottled Duck is the southeastern representative of the Mallard and is relatively common in summer in freshwater and brackish marshes throughout the region. Although they do gather in fairly large flocks during late summer and early fall, Mottled Ducks are less gregarious than other ducks, often occurring in pairs. Both sexes resemble female Mallards. Look for chocolate-colored ducks with tan heads swimming in pairs. The Black Duck's plumage is confusingly similar to that of the Mottled Duck; note the Mottled's paler plumage, especially the crown, supercillium and throat, and the thin white borders to the metallic wing patch. They are best separated by distribution, the Black Duck occurring on the Upper Texas Coast only as an extreme rarity.

Mottled Duck

Alan Murphy, www.AlanMurphyPhotography.com

attract a variety of wintering shore-birds, including Ruddy Turnstone, Black-bellied Plover, Dunlin, and the ubiquitous Willet. Scan the boat docks of newly build homes for roost-ing American Oystercatchers. North Deer Island, a sanctuary for colonial-nesting waterbirds, is visible from the end of 8-Mile Road.

67: Settegast Road

Migrations
Free, Daily
Rating: 2
Stewart Road W to Settegast Road.

Check the freshwater ponds just west of 8-Mile Road for shorebirds such as Semipalmated, Baird's, and White-

rumped sandpipers, large waders, and ducks. The grassy fields along Settegast Road are similar to those along 8-Mile Road, attracting migrat-ing American Golden-Plover (spring), and associated shorebirds.

68: Lafitte's Cove

Migrations
Free, Daily
Rating: 2
Stewart Road W to Eckert Drive 0.1 mile to entrance of Lafitte's Cove subdivision; additional 0.1 mile to parking area at beginning of marsh boardwalk.

Although this site abuts a housing development, its trees are a magnet

RAB/Naturewide Images

Baird's Sandpiper

for migrant landbirds, and the marsh boardwalk and observation gazebo present additional viewing opportunities. This woodlot is compact and can be worked quickly and effectively by one or two people. Its trails pass through an interesting mix of vegetation, including several attractive live oaks, prickly pear, patches of lantana, and a variety of wildflowers. Despite its small size, during favorable weather conditions, activity at this woodland can rival the show at High Island. Do not neglect the low thickets around the site's margin; they can be alive with hummingbirds, Yellow Warblers, Blue Grosbeaks, Orchard Orioles, Baltimore Orioles, and buntings.

TLE

Common Yellowthroat

69: Lafitte's Grove

Migrations
Free, Daily
Rating: 1
Stewart Road W 0.1 mile beyond entrance to Lafitte's Cove (site 68).

Historical accounts suggest that the only naturally occurring trees on Galveston Island grew here at Lafitte's Grove. The Battle of the Three Trees fought here in 1821 between Lafitte's men and Karankawa Indians lends credence to this legend. Supposedly, Lafitte buried a chest of gold at this site, and many treasure hunters have searched for it. The surrounding trees and the small swamp on the seaward side of the monument commemorating the battle now attract a variety of migrants, including many Yellow Warblers and Common Yellowthroats, as well as a few nesting waterbirds. Fall migrants often remain through Christmas along the immediate coast. Throughout the fall and early winter months, check the small oak mottes that border the ponds. This site and the preceding one are examples of small venues that can be highly productive given the right weather conditions.

TLE

Galveston Island State Park

70: Galveston Island State Park

All Seasons
Site fee, Daily
Rating: 2
Stewart Road W; FM 3005 W 0.4
mile to Park Road 66 and Galveston
Island State Park; park extends from
the beach to the bay and may be
entered on north and south sides of
FM 3005.

The bay section of the park offers the
most birding opportunities and is
usually more tranquil than the park's
beach shore. Upon entering from FM
3005, check for migrants or wintering songbirds in the willow groves
bordering the park road. Sedge Wren
and Le Conte's Sparrow winter in
stands of bluestem grasses and low
shrubs. Turn left (west) at the first opportunity and park near the observation tower. Clapper Rail Trail, with its
diversity of seasonally varying waterbirds, is worth walking. If walking
this trail during a summer evening,
watch for fiery flashes of biolumines-
cence in the water below. Small fish
startled by footsteps disturb micro-
scopic plankton, which produces this
glow. Trees across the road from the
parking area should be checked for
migrants and roosting owls. Marshes

bordering the bay abound with resident Seaside and wintering Nelson's
Sharp-tailed sparrows.

Depending on water levels and fish
populations, the marsh's pools may
be jammed with spoonbills, ibis, herons, and egrets. Gull-billed Terns and
Wilson's Plovers lay their eggs on the
flats, and White-tailed Kites nest in
the tall shrubs and small trees. Northern Harrier, once a common year-
round resident, maintains a tenuous
summer hold here. A wait until sunset
is often rewarded with the sight of a
Barn Owl. Barn Owls forage over the
park's open grassland. They can often
be found by going to the grassy area
at Galveston Island State Park on a
clear night, making a squeaking noise
on the back of the hand, and waiting
for an owl to make an appearance.

During winter the Short-eared
Owl occurs here as well. Black Rail,
a rare local breeder, often calls in the
dead of night and is mimicked during
the day by Northern Mockingbirds.
The beach itself sports the usual
complement of Sanderlings, Caspian
and Royal terns, and various gulls.
Picnic facilities, showers, and beach
amenities make this one of the great
sites on the trail, appealing to birders
and nonbirders alike. Obtain a bird
checklist in the park office.

Several interesting and local
butterflies occur in these marshes,
including Great Southern White and
both Salt Marsh and Obscure skip-

Western Pygmy-Blue

pers. Watch carefully for the tiny
Western Pygmy-Blue, one of the
world's smallest butterflies.

71: San Luis Pass

All Seasons
Free, Daily
Rating: 3
From Galveston Island State Park,
continue west on FM 3005 W 11.8
miles to San Luis Pass. Access by
exiting FM 3005 to the north just before toll bridge. At the pavement's end
is a depression that is often flooded.
Check depth before crossing.

RAB/Naturewide Images

Black Terns

The sand at San Luis Pass can be treacherously soft, so drive with extreme caution. Follow firm tire tracks whenever possible. Any wet sediment is likely to be covered by water during a rising tide. A sand road that is usually high and dry parallels the bridge from the beach entrance to the margin of the main channel.

Several smaller roads branch off this main track, allowing access to various parts of the flats. The edge of the main channel is more easily reached by driving under the bridge toward the Gulf, then continuing along the water's edge back toward the bay. This route is popular with anglers, campers, and sunbathers.

San Luis Pass and Bolivar Flats are the two best coastal mudflat viewing areas in Texas. Countless waterbirds pack the sand flats extending into the bay. During migrations and winter, jaegers and some of the rarer gulls have occurred here. Because the flats are extensive, make every attempt to bird them just before, just after, or during high tide. When the tide is out, the feeding and roosting birds may be hundreds of yards from the safest driving area.

Few species of landbirds occur around the flats, but those that do may be present in immense numbers. Opportunities to observe migrating songbirds are limited because many migrate at night or over water. Swallows, however, may be observed

FINDING MAGNIFICENT FRIGATEBIRDS

This large bird has a forked tail and distinctively long wings and can be seen soaring or attacking terns and gulls as it attempts to steal their food. Unlike the neotropical migrants that pass through Texas in spring on their way to breeding grounds in the north, Magnificent Frigatebirds breed in Mexico and extreme southern Florida, after which many individuals, particularly white-headed immature ones, disperse northward. Currently, we don't know which population provides the birds that move north to Texas. Good numbers occur in the heat of summer and early fall. On west Galveston they are especially common, as numbers gather there to pirate food around the tern colonies. They can be seen from the west end of the island as they move out of the bay and into the Gulf to feed, often around shrimp trawlers plying the shallows immediately offshore. At San Luis Pass (site 71), look for them perched on pilings in the bay. Although only occasionally seen from the ferry between Galveston and Bolivar, they can often be seen soaring out over East Bay. Look for these large, distinct birds as they try to steal prey from gulls and terns.

moving northward or southward during the day. During their southward migration, watch for the river of swallows that streams along Galveston Island, only to be bottlenecked at San Luis Pass. In a short span of observation, thousands of individuals may be present. Look for species such as Tree and Bank swallows, both of which are sparse on the Upper Texas Coast.

Both Common Nighthawk and Lesser Nighthawk occur here as well.

During fall migration large insects may share the air lanes with swallows: Monarch butterflies are often common, and dragonflies such as Common Green Darner and Black Saddlebags may occur by the hundreds of thousands.

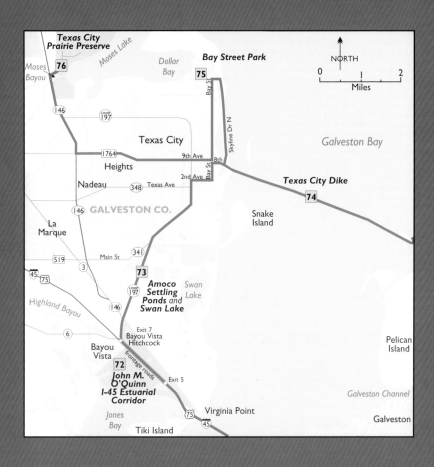

Texas City
Prairie Preserve

Moses
Bayou

76

Moses Lake

Dollar
Bay

Bay Street Park

75

NORTH

0   1   2
Miles

Bay St

146

LOOP
197

Skyline Dr N

Galveston Bay

Texas City

1764

9th Ave

8th

Heights

2nd Ave

Bay St

Texas City Dike

Nadeau   348   Texas Ave

74

GALVESTON CO.

146

Snake
Island

La
Marque

519   341

Main St

3

73

Swan
Lake

45   75

LOOP
197

Amoco
Settling
Ponds and
Swan Lake

Highland Bayou

146

Pelican
Island

6

Exit 7
Bayou Vista
Hitchcock

Bayou
Vista

Frontage roads

72

Exit 5

Galveston Channel

John M.
O'Quinn
I-45 Estuarial
Corridor

Jones
Bay

75

Virginia Point

Galveston

Tiki Island

45

Texas City Loop

The sites on the Texas City Loop follow the southwestern margin of Galveston Bay and are directly west of the tip of the Bolivar Peninsula.

The commercial history of this area began in the late 1800s when facilities were developed for ship and rail transit. Today Texas City and nearby La Marque are residential communities boasting all the trappings of the twenty-first century, including a junior college, Asian fast food, and an outlet mall. To most Texans however, the mention of Texas City conjures up visions of a vast petrochemical complex. Although birding among chemical plants may seem daunting, in reality only one trail site is proximate to the processing facilities. Indeed, these ponds adjacent to the plants of Dow Chemical and Union Carbide host some of our most attractive waterbirds.

Among birders, the loop's best known venue is the Texas City Dike, a five-mile-long finger that points southeast into Bolivar Roads, the shipping lane entry to Galveston Bay and the Houston Ship Channel. Ships and rare birds such as Black-legged Kittiwake and Long-tailed Duck enter Bolivar Roads, a gap between the facing tips of Galveston Island and the Bolivar Peninsula. At the dike's end is a six-hundred-foot-long pier (fee to enter), offering birders and anglers the state's deepest water with pier access. However, the entire length of the dike is productive, with shallow water along the north side and deeper water on the south side.

Although most of the loop's birds are seen often and are fairly numerous, one site gives birders an opportunity to view a critically endangered bird, the Attwater's race of Greater Prairie-Chicken. The global population of this subspecies, now dependent on captive breeding and release programs, hangs on at only a few sites, one of which is the Texas Nature Conservancy's Texas City Prairie Preserve. Birders who are able to plan in advance should seriously consider spending a spring morning at this site.

A visit to the John M. O'Quinn I-45 Estuarial Corridor provides a glimpse of habitat being returned to Galveston Bay. As the bulldozed islands are smoothed and the bay's natural processes take over, the area is again coming to be inhabited by a greater array of plants and wildlife. Another site that is improving with age is Bay Street Park. Here, butterflies and hummingbirds are being attracted to a new garden, channels, and ponds. Scattered clumps of shrubs and trees attract a variety of landbirds and waterbirds.

72: John M. O'Quinn I-45 Estuarial Corridor

All Seasons
Free, Daily
Rating: 2
To bird toward Houston via sites on upper Galveston Bay: I-45 N 5.0 miles, take frontage road exit at mile 5. Work the frontage road along bay's edge to TX 146.

The marshes from Virginia Point on Galveston Bay north to Texas Highway 146 are part of the John M. O'Quinn I-45 Estuarial Corridor, a habitat corridor being developed by a municipal plan known as Scenic Galveston. The plan calls for removal of most existing structures, and the entire area is being returned to its original wetland state. The marshes can be birded from the service roads bordering both sides of I-45 between exits 5 and 7. An observation area with a parking lot, a short path to the bay's edge, and a lone shade tree are available on the south side of I-45, just southeast of the Bayou Vista/ Hitchcock exit (Texas Highway 6). In order to reach this parking area, exit toward Hitchcock, make a U-turn, return to I-45, and go just a short distance toward Galveston along the frontage road. This area can be full

Short-billed Dowitcher

RAB./Naturewide Images

RAB/Naturewide Images

Lesser Scaup

of Short-billed Dowitchers, Lesser Yellowlegs, Black-bellied Plovers, and other mudpeckers. Photographers take note: traffic-acclimated herons, egrets, spoonbills, and rails may be seen feeding within a few feet of the highway. As the tide and its attendant fish populations change, so do the bird assemblages. Watch the deeper pools for grebes, cormorants, and diving ducks. Long-tailed Duck has been seen here.

73: Amoco Settling Ponds and Swan Lake

All Seasons
Free, Daily
Rating:
From TX 146 N Loop 197 N 1.3 miles to ponds on left and lake on right.

The ponds to the east and west may be viewed from the shoulder of Loop 197. These ponds attract shorebirds and waterfowl at all seasons. During winter, watch for diving ducks such as Bufflehead, Lesser Scaup, Canvasback, and Redhead. Greater Scaup and Horned Grebe, both uncommon visitors to coastal impoundments, have occurred here. The pond on the east side of the road, Swan Lake, can be a genuine hotspot, as it seems to attract everything from Roseate Spoonbill and Brown Pelican to unusual wintering shorebirds. Here even nonbirders pull over to comment on the bird diversity of the ponds. In spring, Swan Lake is a good bet for Wilson's Phalarope, and Stilt Sandpiper, primarily a spring visitor, is regular here during winter. The northern portion of this pond is close to the road and abuts a channel. Here, Neotropic and Double-crested cormorants are often present in large numbers, with Double-crested Cormorant occurring mainly in winter; Black-crowned Night-Herons and other large wading birds are also often seen. On winter mornings, there may be considerable numbers of Snow and Ross's geese overhead.

74: Texas City Dike

Winter
Free, Daily
Rating: 3
North on Loop 197; Texas Ave/2nd

Ave E 0.5 mile; Bay St. N 0.7 mile; 8th Ave turn right to reach dike.

In winter the five-mile drive along the Texas City Dike is always worthwhile, both as a place to photograph waterbirds and as a place to search for rarities, which have included the Upper Texas Coast's first Greater Flamingo. Birding is good in summer, although the species diversity is not as great. Magnificent Frigatebird, Least Tern, and other visitors occur here. Common Loons winter in good numbers, occasionally feeding right along the south side of the dike. Pacific Loon is rare and Red-throated Loon rarer still. Red-breasted Merganser, cormorants, pelicans, and other water-

Herring Gull

birds are generally plentiful. Fishing boats attract huge flocks of birds as deck hands sort the day's catch, and jaegers may appear among the scavenging hordes. Forster's Terns are ubiquitous, and Bonaparte's Gull (regular), Franklin's Gull (uncommon), and Black-legged Kittiwake (rare) may be seen among the more common Ring-billed, Laughing, and Herring gulls. Glaucous, Thayer's, Great Black-backed, and Lesser Black-backed gulls and other low-density visitors can always occur here, so scan carefully. Look for American Oyster-catcher among the shorebirds loafing on the spoil islands along the north side of the dike. Ruddy Turnstones work the rubble piles at the water's edge. Watch for bottlenose dolphins in the deeper water on the south side of the dike.

RAB/Naturewide Images

Merlin

75: Bay Street Park

Migrations, Winter
Free, Daily
Rating: 2
From base of dike, take Skyline Drive N to metal gate adjacent to pumping station; turn W and drive a short distance to Bay Street and park.

Sprague's Pipit winters in the closely cropped grass on the shoulders of this hurricane levee. After about half a mile, notice an observation building

on the left. This attractive structure is a scale model of the Halfmoon Shoal Lighthouse that was present 2.5 miles off Texas City in the late nineteenth century. Inside the ga-zebo-like structure are panels with maps, stories about Texas City and its nautical history, and some bird information. During winter, the lake that may be viewed from this platform often has Redheads, Buffleheads, and large flocks of Ruddy Ducks. Bird here with a scope or by walking down to the lake's edge. Watch for a wintering American Kestrel; Merlin and Peregrine Falcon occur here too. Continue along the road until reaching a metal gate adjacent to a pumping station. Turn west and drive a very short distance to Bay Street and Bay Street Park. Bay Street eventually circles back to the south, and the park is located to the east. Continuing straight at the gate leads to the 810-acre Dollar Bay tract of the Nature Conservancy's Texas City Prairie Preserve. Access is on foot only; check with the preserve office for additional information (see site 76).

The north section of Bay Street Park, also known as the Thomas S. Mackey Nature Center, was developed with the assistance of the Boy Scouts and Girl Scouts. There are bathrooms and paved trails with wheelchair access. The butterfly and hummingbird garden at this site was begun by the Texas Department of Transportation but was resurrected and extensively modified by residents of Texas City. The maturing plants make the site more and more attractive to insects; visits can produce a variety of butterflies, including hundreds of skippers representing various species. During spring and fall watch for migrating Ruby-throated Hummingbirds, and check the garden throughout the winter months for Rufous, Black-chinned, and Broad-tailed hummingbirds as well as the occasional rarity that comes through the park.

Amoco has provided funding to modify thirty-five acres of the park with improvements that include clearing introduced Chinese tallow trees and replacing them with native species. New shrub plantings provide additional habitat for wintering birds. Nature trails meandering through the park cross several wooden bridges and pass aquatic habitats that attract a few waterbirds and many dragonflies. The park has active Purple Martin houses.

76: Texas City Prairie Preserve, Nature Conservancy of Texas

All Seasons
Phone for access: (409) 945-4677
Rating: 2
TX 146 N, cross Moses Bayou, and turn right into preserve.

This twenty-five-hundred-acre sanctuary features rare coastal prairie habitat and is one of the last remaining sites supporting a population of critically endangered Attwater's Prairie-Chickens. The refuge is quite new, having been established in 1995. Mobil and Exxon (then separate), Enron, and BP provided funds for property acquisition and improvements. Because of the prairie-chickens, access to most of the sanctuary is restricted. Some of the prairie and wetland property along the bayfront, as well as the Dollar Bay tract across Moses Bayou, may be reached by car or on foot, but permission is needed.

Greater (Attwater's) Prairie-Chicken

Clifford E. Shackelford

An oak motte at the north end of the refuge attracts spring migrants. During early spring, several local clubs offer organized tours to view the prairie-chickens. Contact the refuge manager for details about either tours or independent visits.

Although this site is best known for its remaining nesting population of Attwater's Prairie-Chickens, the refuge bird list available at the office tallies nearly 250 species that have been recorded on the property, including the majority of the eastern waterbirds, warblers, and sparrows. Again, because various portions of it require special permission to enter, call before attempting to visit the preserve.

Texas City Prairie Preserve
The Nature Conservancy of Texas
4702 Highway 146 North
Texas City, TX 77590
Office: (409) 945-4677

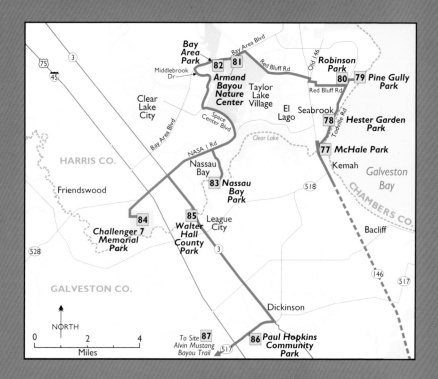

Clear Lake Loop

The Clear Lake Loop concentrates on a number of sites in Harris and Galveston counties, eventually ending in Brazoria County. Although brackish waterbird habitats are an important aspect of this loop, there are many opportunities here to enjoy both woodland and prairie birds.

The bayside towns in the Clear Lake region, including Seabrook, Kemah, El Lago, and Nassau Bay, are well known to sailors, anglers, and boaters.

This side of Galveston Bay provides a different vantage point for viewing the bay's wildlife communities. In general, this area has a higher diversity of habitats than on the coast, which helps explain the high numbers recorded during annual bird counts. Wetland areas, both freshwater and saltwater, pine woodlands, and bay waters all produce excellent habitat for birds. Seabrook is proud of Pine Gully Park on the bayfront, where saltmarsh habitat traversed by a trail and boardwalk can produce both Clapper and King Rails and sometimes an alligator. Buteos such as Red-tailed Hawk occur in winter.

Historically, this part of Galveston Bay served as the focal point for birding on the Upper Texas Coast. The twin effects of development and the higher profile of venues such as High Island, Bolivar, Galveston, and San Luis Pass have diverted birders to those better known locations. Most birders nowadays head straight for the Gulf Coast. The fact remains, however, that this loop presents numerous opportunities for both waterbirds and migrant landbirds. With good timing and a bit of luck, exploring these sites can produce excellent birding. As with other segments of the Great Texas Coastal Birding Trail, no spot is too minor to check during migrations. For birders who are under time constraints, this complex of sites makes an excellent alternative to the longer treks to Galveston or Bolivar.

Anchoring the loop is Armand Bayou Nature Center, the country's largest urban nature center. Its activities are diverse, ranging from prairie restoration to cheese making demonstrations. Twenty-five hundred acres of habitat offer birders a wide variety of nesting birds and migrants, and the center draws naturalists of all ages and skill levels from Houston and beyond. Visitors may participate in a variety of training programs ranging from nature appreciation to field biology.

Seabrook has a sister-city agreement with Santa Cruz in the Galápagos Islands. Cultural, ecological, and exchange connections between these cities are building.

77: McHale Park

All Seasons
Free, Daily
Rating: 1
From TX 146 in Texas City, proceed north to the Kemah Bridge. After crossing the bridge, immediately exit right. Circle back south on Waterfront Drive, cross Todville Road, and enter McHale Park.

This park, one of the smallest on the trail, is a good spot from which to view the western shore of Galveston Bay. From the slightly elevated observation platform, scan the pilings and nearshore waters. During winter, gulls, terns, herons, egrets, and Double-crested Cormorants occur here. However, the park's chief attraction is pelicans. Flocks of both Brown and American White pelicans have colonized the area. Between October and April, expect large numbers of these fascinating birds all along the

American White Pelican

RAB/Naturewide Images

shoreline. Other coastal areas host high concentrations of them, but the distinctive component here is the proliferation of pilings along the shoreline, creating superb perches for the pelicans and allowing cautious birders and photographers to get relatively close. The adjacent salt marshes should be checked as well for herons and egrets. A Great Black-backed Gull wintered in this area for several years.

RAB/Naturewide Images

Little Wood Satyr

78: Hester Garden Park

All Seasons, Migrations best
Free, Daily
Rating: 1
From TX 146, exit McHale Park and drive north (right) on Todville 1.7 miles to Hester Garden Park.

Migrants crowd these woodlands, which are often underbirded as birders now haunt the better known migrant traps at Bolivar Peninsula and Galveston Island. Freshwater wetland and woodland habitats here attract a good diversity of species. Woodpeckers and Barn Owl both occur here.

Hester Garden Park contains an impressive variety of trees and shrubs; it was once a commercial nursery and some plants are introduced, like the bamboos. After walking a short distance down the trail beyond the futuristic drinking fountain and picnic table, watch on the left for a short pier. Approach slowly and look down at the channel's edge, where male fiddler crabs seductively wave an exaggerated claw back and forth at the smaller females. Check the live oaks in late fall and winter for Brown Thrasher, Hermit Thrush, Blue-headed Vireo, and several warblers. In spring, watch the pool margins for Prothonotary Warbler and waterthrushes. Many of the plantings are evergreen and attractive to lingering insectivores, so scrutinize the flocks and *pissh* for less common birds, such as Northern Parula, Black-throated Green Warbler, and Yellow-throated Warbler. Because of the habitat diversity and various water characteristics, this park should be productive for both dragonflies and butterflies. Watch for woodland butterfly species such as Gemmed and Little Wood satyrs.

Due to its location close to the bay, temperature at this park is moderate and it rarely freezes. Tropical flora planted over the years provides habitat for lingering neotropicals, wintering warblers, hummingbirds, and flycatchers. As with downtown Galveston, simply birding neighborhood yards in winter can yield interesting sightings. Take care not to trespass or impede traffic.

79: Pine Gully Park

All Seasons
Site fee, Daily
Rating: 1
From McHale Park (site 77) continue

Black-throated Green Warbler

RAB/Naturewide Images

north on Todville Road 1.4 miles, then east (right) on Pine Gully Road into Pine Gully Park.

This pleasant fifty-two-acre multiuse facility offers a fine venue from which to scan the shallows of Galveston Bay. The trees within the park are perfectly situated to intercept migrating landbirds. Migration in fall here can be particularly good because birds that are migrating south to cross the Gulf of Mexico stage in these woodlands before crossing the bay. The birds mass here until the wind shifts to favor their southward crossing of the Gulf. The whole area was a prime birding venue in the 1930s and '40s because of its combination of woodlands and bayshore habitats, which remain excellent places to see birds. The nature trail enters the deep woods, then emerges to reach a short boardwalk over a marsh that attracts Swamp Sparrow and many of the local waterbirds, including resident rails. During winter, a large mixed-species foraging flock and several species of woodpeckers (including Pileated) are generally evident where the trail passes the local cemetery. A fairly long pier allows birders and photographers a different perspective of the shore and associated birds, including Osprey, White Pelican, and various gulls. Periodic wildflower plantings enhance

RAB/Naturewide Images

Great Southern White

butterfly diversity. The shallow lower reach of the lovely bayou called Pine Gully is a tidal creek. Fresh water entering at the upstream end of the park forms a deeper section where alligators are sometimes seen. This park is a good starting point for exploring Seabrook's network of several miles of hiking trails.

80: Robinson Park

Migrations
Free, Daily
Rating: 2
Robinson Park is at the intersection of Todville and Red Bluff roads; watch for an attractively landscaped gazebo by the parking lot.

Robinson Park contains approximately twenty acres of old oaks, with a few pines and a dense understory. The park trail connects with Pine Gully Park to the north and Hester Garden Park to the south, so visitors who are turning up birds at the one park have every incentive, particularly during migration, to walk the trail. There are grassy openings in the woodland edge and several irregular trails that enter the woods. The entire woodland edge and the available openings are good habitat for a variety of butterflies. The open, surfaced trail follows a channel that is variously flooded or has isolated pools attracting a few large waders and a nice assortment of dragonflies. The surfaced, manicured trails are accessible to the disabled.

Armand Bayou Nature Center

81: Armand Bayou Nature Center

All Seasons
Site fee, Tuesday–Sunday
Rating: 3
From the intersection of Todville and
Red Bluff roads, take Red Bluff W
1.5 miles; dogleg right and then left,
twice (part of Red Bluff is along Old
146); cross TX 146 and continue on
Red Bluff NW 2.8 miles, then take
Bay Area Blvd. W 0.4 mile to nature
center.

This site is the ideal form of urban
greenspace: large, intact, and pos-

sessing a variety of habitats, the
nature center's twenty-five hundred
acres host a superb variety of birdlife.
Estuarine bayou wetland, hardwood
riparian forest, and tall grass prairie
provide great year-round birding. The
center's grasslands are productive
for a variety of sparrows; Field Sparrow and Savannah Sparrow as well
as harder-to-find target birds such as
Le Conte's Sparrow all winter here.
Sedge Wren can often be heard chattering along the entrance road. No
less than fourteen sparrow species
have been identified, which means
that the center is a great place to

study this potentially confounding but extraordinarily interesting group of birds. Wild Turkeys are present on both banks of the bayou. Two bison are maintained in a five-acre enclosure. The center is also an excellent resource for finding out about recent sightings in the area.

Among the many reptile species found at the center are flat-headed snake, rough earth snake, Texas brown snake, marsh brown snake, Mississippi ring-necked snake, eastern garter snake, Gulf Coast ribbon snake, diamond-backed water snake, yellow-bellied water snake, and blotched water snake.

Opportunities for nature photographers are virtually limitless due to the plentiful amphibians, butterflies, and dragonflies. Armand Bayou offers an unusual array of natural history experiences. These include Saturday morning guided canoe tours; pontoon boat cruises that may include breakfast or be scheduled at night to view the bayou's mammals, night birds, and aquatic life; owl prowls; nighttime hayrides; and a variety of bird walks. For schedules, check the center's Web site at http://www.abnc.org.

Wild Turkey

82: Bay Area Park

All Seasons
Free, Daily
Rating: 1
From Armand Bayou Nature Center (site 81), continue Bay Area Blvd. W 0.8 mile and turn left into Bay Area Park.

This Harris County site is located on Armand Bayou. Parking areas along the loop drive, a boardwalk, and a viewing deck all offer unobstructed views of the bayou. Cormorants and summering Anhingas are expected, as well as the usual assortment of large waders. In winter, hordes of Laughing Gulls and a few Ring-billed Gulls join the motley flock of park ducks and geese to accept handouts. The park's wooded edge has Pine Warbler, chickadees, and titmice. Yellow-bellied Sapsucker and other woodpeckers, both kinglets, Orange-crowned Warbler, Blue-gray Gnatcatcher, and other migrants join them in winter. During migration and winter, watch for Osprey; Black Vultures may be encountered at any time of the year. A canoe and kayak launch site is available for those who want to explore the bay area by water.

83: Nassau Bay Park

All Seasons
Free, Daily
Rating: 1
From Bay Area Park (site 82) take Bay Area Blvd. W 1.1 miles; Middlebrook Drive E (left) 1.6 miles; Space Center Blvd. S 1.8 miles; NASA Road 1 W (right) 1.0 mile; Upper Bay Road S (left) 1.5 miles to Nassau Bay Park, scanning the waters on left.

This city park consists of a grassy recreational area flanked by two saltwater coves. Likely birds include common species such as Laughing Gull, Spotted Sandpiper, American Coot, Ruddy Duck, Great Blue Heron, Great Egret, and Tricolored Heron. During migration the waters can be filled with ducks and pelicans, so a quick check here is always worthwhile. Large numbers of commoner birds such as Laughing Gull provide an excellent opportunity to study variability within a single species. Differences in age, the amount of time that a bird has been in a particular plumage, and normal variation between individuals provide a host of characteristics to note when looking at gulls. Seasonal changes in bill color and leg color add to the number of interesting variations presented by these birds.

TLE

Ruddy Duck

84: Challenger 7 Memorial Park

All Seasons
Free, Daily
Rating: 2
TX 3 S to NASA 1 Rd; cross I-45,
where NASA 1 Rd. becomes Wilson
Rd.; continue W on Wilson 0.5 mile;
West NASA Blvd. S 0.9 mile; take left
fork and then turn into Challenger 7
Memorial Park.

This park combines very open and
very dense habitats and consequently
has a good variety of birds. When
entering the park, watch during
spring and summer for Scissor-tailed
Flycatcher; listen in winter and spring
for the chattering of Sedge Wren in
the dry, red prairie grasses. Le Conte's
and Henslow's sparrows should be
present in this same habitat. Killdeer and American Robin are often
abundant on the lawns; watch for the
extremely rare Varied Thrush among
the robins, distinguished by its breast
band, bold wing pattern, and striking
eyeline.

At the large parking lot with
buildings on the right, watch for
the entrance to the nature trail. A
second entrance, also on the right,
is close to the boat ramp just a bit
farther along. These nature trails are
paved and provide wheelchair and
all-season access. They pass through
dense thickets with wintering Brown
Thrasher, White-throated Sparrow,

RAB/Naturewide Images

Gray Catbird

and Northern Cardinal; Orange-crowned, Pine, and Yellow-rumped warblers; and the occasional Gray Catbird. Just beyond the Mother Earth ecosculpture, an attractive boardwalk enters low-lying forest and terminates at a shaded platform with a marsh view. By late February or early March, snowy white masses of trifoliate orange blossoms accent this woodland as the rich scent perfumes portions of the boardwalk. This barbed-wire-like citrus tree, a native of China and Korea, is widespread in East Texas, where it is used in container gardens and planted in rows to make dense living fences. Its fruits, the size of a ping-pong ball, are eaten by a variety of birds and mammals.

Watch for Carolina Wren, White-eyed Vireo, and seasonal songbirds such as Northern Parula, Prothonotary Warbler, and Yellow-throated Vireo. At the boat ramp along Clear Creek, sit at a moss-shaded picnic table and scan for kingfishers and waders. In open stretches of the park, watch for locally nesting White-tailed Hawk and White-tailed Kite. Red-shouldered Hawk is present in the wooded sections.

85: Walter Hall County Park

Migrations, Winter
Free, Daily Closes at 10:00 P.M.
Rating: 1
From intersection of TX 3 and NASA
Road 1, take TX 3 S 2.0 miles to
Walter Hall County Park on right.

This site is primarily a multiuse facility, but along Clear Creek the moss-covered trees can be hopping with Yellow-rumped, Pine, and Orange-crowned warblers. Pileated Woodpeckers are frequently heard and can be found with little difficulty. The loud tattoo of this bird's large and powerful bill distinguishes it from all other locally occurring woodpeckers. The bayou provides habitat for herons and egrets. Pay attention to the foraging actions of any white egrets; they are often a good clue to distinguishing between similar species. During spring or fall migration, a visit here should be productive. Among older birders, this site is best known for a Varied Thrush that appeared in 1965.

Pine Warbler

86: Paul Hopkins Community Park

Migrations, Winter
Free, Daily
Rating: 1
From TX 3 in Dickinson, take FM 517 W 1.0 mile to Paul Hopkins Community Park on left. The park can be entered on either side of the bridge.

The nature trail and observation platforms enhance access to the woodland and bayou. Although the park is small, it is sandwiched between wooded neighborhoods and the habitat remains attractive. Winter mixed-species flocks can be entertaining and should always be checked carefully for the presence of unusual species. Feeding flocks, when encountered, can generally be called into extremely close range with loud *pisshing* sounds. Proximate views of Yellow-rumped Warbler, Carolina

FINDING URBAN BIRDS

RAB/Naturewide Images

Inca Dove

Urban Doves: The northern spread of White-winged and Inca doves, and the western expansion of Eurasian Collared-Dove has been facilitated by the growth of cities. These urban islands offer spilled grain, exotic gardens, trash, and feeders where birds find year-round nourishment. More mature neighborhoods in particular present birds with nesting platforms in trees and buildings, in place of the prairies and marshes that once covered this area. In older Houston neighborhoods such as West University and Bellaire, it is not unusual to have five or six species of doves congregate at a feeder. Troll these neighborhoods and search the utility lines for White-winged Dove and Eurasian Collared-Dove. The rattling flight noise of Inca Dove is distinctive; having learned it, you will be surprised how many of these birds you locate by ear.

Mulberry Birds: Several of the more colorful spring migrants are attracted to fruiting mulberry trees, which have variable but characteristically lobed, dark green leaves and red berries. Check these whenever possible during spring migration. This complex of birds includes Baltimore Oriole, Rose-breasted Grosbeak, Summer Tanager, Scarlet Tanager, Indigo Bunting, migrant thrushes, and Gray Catbird. The gardens at Boy Scout Woods (site 55) and Smith Oaks (site 52), the boardwalk at Sea Rim State Park (site 27), and residential neighborhoods in coastal towns are all places to seek out these trees. Mulberries concentrate migrants and provide an observation post at which to study them at leisure. They also provide excellent photo vantage points.

Winter Hummingbirds: As coastal communities have matured, the exotic vegetation in cities such as Houston, Galveston, and Lake Jackson has matured with them, creating an artificial forest that attracts and holds hummingbirds through winter. This human-made forest provides hummingbirds with insects and winter-blooming flowers. To add to the attractiveness of this environment, in the last twenty years urbanites have added hummingbird feeders in huge numbers. Large communities also act as heat sinks, because their buildings and trees maintain warmer temperatures than in the surrounding open areas. Such heat sinks enhance the survival of wintering birds, especially during inclement weather.

Consequently, birders now have opportunities to see an impressive variety of wintering hummingbirds and to attract them to urban yards. The climate here favors ornamentals that produce nectar, a number of

TLE

Buff-bellied Hummingbird

which flower through mild winters. Although the Upper Texas Coast has only one breeding species, Ruby-throated Hummingbird, at least a dozen hummingbird species have occurred here in winter, with Rufous, Buff-bellied, Black-chinned, Broad-tailed, and Ruby-throated hummingbirds being regulars. Records for Allen's, Calliope, Blue-throated, Violet-crowned, and Anna's hummingbirds and Green Violet-ear make the viewing possibilities in winter quite impressive. In other parts of the country people take their feeders down in the fall—but on the Texas coast fall is the time to put them up. Rufous Hummingbirds usually begin to arrive by the third week of July, when Ruby-throated Hummingbirds are still present. Black-chinned Hummingbirds join them not long after. Thus feeders can attract these birds year-round.

Rare Bird Alerts: These taped messages are an important information source for those intent on seeing hummingbirds in the area. From late December through late January contact the Christmas Bird Count organizers, especially in Lake Jackson. Feeders are at homes and not necessarily at trail sites, so permission is often required to access the property. Russ Pitman Park in Bellaire (site 92) is usually loaded with hummingbirds. Almost all winter sightings are feeder birds or are associated with large gardens such as those at High Island or Bay Street Park (site 75). In spring, Ruby-throated Hummingbirds can be found near honeysuckle or any unkempt woodland edge or hedgerow.

Some hummers exhibit strong fidelity to a single feeder and may guard it fiercely. Others work a series of feeders, and still others will not come to feeders at all. Which feeders are involved will determine where to see the birds. For additional information on attracting and feeding hummingbirds, check the Texas Parks and Wildlife Department Web site.

Chickadee, Northern Cardinal, Pine Warbler, and several species of large waders along the creek's margin add to this site's appeal.

87: Alvin Mustang Bayou Trail

Migrations, Winter
Free, Daily, but as yet undeveloped
Rating: 1
From I-45, FM 517 W about 10 miles to Alvin; TX 35 S (left) a couple of hundred feet, bear right onto TX 6, and continue 1.0 mile; Business 35 S 0.3 mile, cross the tracks, and turn left on Willis Street. There is an old railroad station and a couple of rows of recently planted trees where the trailhead is planned.

En route to Alvin, check the grazed fields flanking FM 517 for migrating Upland Sandpiper and Long-billed Curlew. Alvin is an ideal base from which to explore Brazos Bend State Park (site 117), offering several reasonably priced motels and restaurants, and easy access to Interstate 45 to proceed north to Houston or south to Galveston. Brazos Bend State Park is about half an hour's drive from here. To get there go south on Business 35, west on FM 1462, and north on FM 762, turning right at the sign for the park.

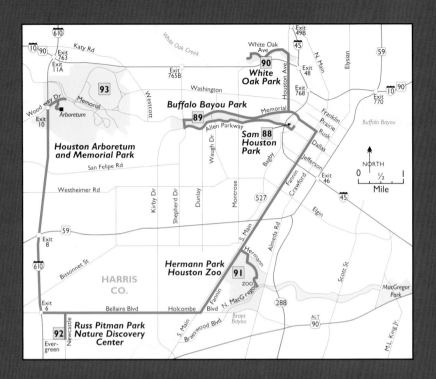

93 Houston Arboretum and Memorial Park

89 Buffalo Bayou Park

90 White Oak Park

88 Sam Houston Park

91 Hermann Park Houston Zoo

92 Russ Pitman Park Nature Discovery Center

White Oak Creek

Katy Rd

Exit 763
Exit 11A

Exit 765B

Washington

Woodway Dr

Memorial

Exit 10

Arboretum

Westcott

San Felipe Rd

Westheimer Rd

Kirby Dr

Shepherd Dr

Dunlay

Waugh Dr

Montrose

Allen Parkway

White Oak Ave

Houston Ave

Memorial

Exit 49B

Exit 48

Exit 768

N. Main

Elysian

Exit 770

Buffalo Bayou

Franklin
Prairie
Rusk
Dallas

Bagby

Jefferson

Exit 46

Crawford

Fannin

Elgin

527

Scott St

MacGregor Park

NORTH

0   ½   1
Mile

Exit 59

Exit 8

Bissonnet St

HARRIS CO.

Exit 6

Bellaire Blvd

Holcombe Blvd

S. Main

Hermann

N. MacGregor

Fannin

Almeda Rd

ZOO

288

Brays Bayou

Braeswood Blvd

ALT 90

M. L. King Jr.

Newcastle

Evergreen

White Oak Park

Buffalo Bayou Park

Sam Houston Park

Hermann Park Houston Zoo

Houston Arboretum and Memorial Park

Russ Pitman Park Nature Discovery Center

Buffalo Bayou Loop

Many people react with disbelief at learning that the counties surrounding Houston have an aggregate bird list greater than that of most states in the nation. This loop offers several sites for visiting birders who may have traveled to Houston on business but do not have enough time to get down to the coast. Some locations are within walking distance or a short drive from downtown Houston and the Texas Medical Center. Many can be reached by the city's network of bus routes. These sites are also particularly appealing to local birders who walk a regular beat to get their daily fix of feathers.

Given its huge population size and sprawling metropolitan area, Houston is surprisingly green. Many visitors flying into the city anticipate the dry scrub of West Texas and are amazed at the forested landscape. Since the Allen brothers founded Houston in 1836, upwards of a million native and exotic trees, including pines, sweetgum, southern catalpa, oaks of various species, tulip poplar, magnolia, redbud, hackberry, cherry laurel, and dozens of others have been planted, creating an open forest that has crept outward from the city's boggy core. Not surprisingly, birds such as Yellow-crowned Night-Heron, Red-shouldered Hawk, Swainson's Hawk, Eastern Screech-Owl, Barred Owl, Common Nighthawk, Pileated Woodpecker, Red-headed Woodpecker, Red-bellied Woodpecker, Brown-headed Nuthatch, and Pine Warbler now nest within the state's largest metropolitan center.

During migration, orioles, grosbeaks, tanagers, and warblers flit through urban yards, while yellowlegs, Spotted Sandpipers, and other shorebirds forage on the algae-covered margins of the city's concrete-lined bayous, and hundreds of Mississippi Kites linger to feed aloft on dragonflies. In winter, feeders and ornamental plantings attract orioles, warblers, and nearly a dozen species of hummingbirds. Mixed flocks of woodland birds roam the mature trees of older, well-established neighborhoods.

This loop begins downtown with several sites adjacent to Buffalo Bayou, the waterway that widens to the east into Houston's Ship Channel.

The bayou is a conduit not only for ships but also for many estuarine species, those that live at the interface between fresh water and sea water. Do not be surprised to see an Osprey pursuing jumping mullet, or a Snowy Egret tussling with a feisty blue crab. Many of the area's hundreds of miles of waterways can be seen throughout the city, ranging from huge stormwater runoff conduits to muddy drainage ditches lined with crawfish chimneys. Watch their banks for soft-shelled turtles, shorebirds, White Ibis, various herons and egrets, and the many night-herons that nest in town.

88: Sam Houston Park

Migrations
Free, Daily
Rating: 2
Begin city birding at Sam Houston Park, opposite the Texaco Heritage Plaza at 1100 Bagby. On weekends there is parking along Allen Parkway on the park's edge.

This nineteen-acre park, with its mature oaks and pecans, offers refuge among the skyscrapers to both birds and Houstonians. The Environmental Institute of Houston, Heritage Society, National Fish and Wildlife Foundation, and several other groups have constructed a small but attractive freshwater wetland bordering the park's lake. Green Herons flit among the shrubbery bordering the pond, and Great Egrets prey on the park's fishes and turtles before the day's first in-line skaters roll in. Most of the pond's numerous turtles are red-eared sliders, more habituated to people and more easily photographed than their wary country cousins.

These wetlands and the adjacent small lake have hosted several locally rare dragonflies, including Neon Skimmer and Red-tailed Pennant. Just up the grassy rise from the small lake are several restored historical buildings. Among them, an attractive butterfly garden of native flora has been established, and most of the plants are labeled. Look for fliers about the plants utilized in the garden. Oaks around City Hall are also worth checking during spring migration.

89: Buffalo Bayou Park

Migrations, Winter and Summer potentially interesting
Free, Daily
Rating: 1
From Sam Houston Park, go west on Allen Parkway 0.4 mile. There is parking on the south side of the bayou at Eleanor Tinsley Park.

Buffalo Bayou Park extends from downtown Houston west to Shepherd Drive. A hike-and-bike trail borders

RAB/Naturewide Images

Neon Skimmer

the bayou; a rougher trail follows the margin of the riparian vegetation. A few species of herons and egrets are generally present. At all seasons, but especially during migration, the trees, shrubs and weedy edges along the bayou attract songbirds.

90: White Oak Park

Migrations, Winter
Free, Daily
Rating: 1
From Memorial E (toward downtown); exit after going under a small bridge and take Houston Avenue N (left) 1.2 miles; bear W (left) at fork onto White Oak Drive, and scan for parking space on left.

The most attractive habitat in White Oak Park is the stretch of woods around a pond, just after turning left on White Oak Drive. Nesting Yellow-crowned Night-Heron, Green Heron, and Black-crowned Night-Heron occur in the restored wetland.

This park is sometimes messy, but do not be discouraged by the litter-bugs. A number of eastern woodland species reside here. During winter, watch for Downy and Red-bellied woodpeckers, Northern Flicker, Orange-crowned and Yellow-rumped warblers, American Robin, and American Goldfinch. Eastern fox squirrels are numerous. During any spring morning, especially a cold or rainy one, this park could be seething with migrants. By late February pollinating

RAB/Naturewide Images

Green Heron

insects are present, including a few butterflies. Summer brings a good selection of butterflies and dragonflies to the weedy wooded margins. The bayou flowing past the park is lined with concrete but has many fish and invertebrates, so it attracts herons and egrets, wintering and migrating yellowlegs, and Spotted and Least sandpipers. Look carefully for other shorebirds as well.

Stude Park, about one mile farther west on White Oak Drive and mainly a recreational facility, and Woodland Park just north of White Oak Park, are worth a brief visit, particularly during migration.

91: Hermann Park and Houston Zoo

Winter for waterfowl, Spring for zoo bird activity, All Seasons for resident species
Site Fee for the zoo, no charge for park visits, available daily
Rating: 2
Going E on Memorial Drive (which becomes Rusk Avenue), take Fannin Street S (right) 2.8 miles; left on Hermann Drive 0.1 mile and right at stop sign for 0.1 mile through Houston Museum of Natural Science parking lot. Turn left and follow the park road 0.5 mile to the zoo parking lot entrance on right.

Adjacent to one of the world's largest and most advanced medical complexes, the Houston Zoo and other venues in Hermann Park attest to the city's concern for inspirational as well as medicinal therapy. The zoo and its surroundings have undergone significant changes in recent years. The muddy margin of the lake adjacent to the zoo parking lot has been stabilized and reshaped, additional trees have been planted along its perimeter, and trails, islands, bridges, and wetlands have been added. New piers improve access for birders, photographers, and casual visitors. Even at the height of construction hundreds of Black-bellied Whistling-Ducks as well as several wintering Ring-necked Ducks and a few herons were present. The zoo maintains a widely acclaimed endangered species breeding program and has both indoor and outdoor exhibits—including a walk-through aviary—that will be of interest to most birders.

RAB/Naturewide Images

Black-bellied Whistling-Duck

The proximity of the park to the city's medical and business centers makes it a convenient side trip for urban birding. During summer look for typical species such as Chimney Swift and Barn Swallow; Red-headed, Red-bellied, and Downy woodpeckers; Carolina Chickadee and Tufted Titmouse; Inca, White-winged, and Mourning doves and Eurasian Collared-Dove; and Blue Jay, Common and Great-tailed grackles, and Great Crested Flycatcher. In winter the swifts and swallows depart and Eastern Phoebes replace the nesting flycatchers. Kinglets, Brown Creeper, Pine Warbler, and Yellow-rumped Warbler join the roving bands of chickadees and titmice. On the lakes and reflecting pools, Ring-billed Gulls, Black-bellied Whistling-Ducks, and Wood Ducks are common, joined by an assortment of other waterfowl that includes Redhead, Ring-necked Duck, the occasional Red-breasted Merganser, Mallard, Ruddy Duck, Lesser Scaup, and rarely

Orange-crowned Warbler at hummingbird feeder

RAB/Naturewide Images

go S (left) on Newcastle 0.5 mile to Russ Pitman Park at the intersection with Evergreen. There are parking lots at both ends of the property.

Leaving the zoo, the nearby Rice University campus has nesting Yellow-crowned Night-Heron, House Finch, American Robin, and in summer a few Bronzed Cowbirds.

Mature hardwoods and conifers and additional plantings in this established neighborhood provide fruits and flowers that attract birds and insects. A seed feeder at the north end of Russ Pitman Park attracts eastern fox and gray squirrels, Blue Jay, and various members of the grackle/ blackbird clan. Nectar feeders maintained by nature center staff are magnets for wintering hummingbirds: Buff-bellied, Ruby-throated, Black-chinned, Broad-tailed, and Rufous hummingbirds have all occurred here in recent years. Eastern Screech-Owls often nest on the property and in the surrounding neighborhoods. This is one of the best winter hummingbird sites on the Great Texas Coastal Birding Trail. The neighborhood has significant mature exotic landscaping that attracts the hummingbirds. The park's feeders then lure the hummingbirds away from the plants that brought them there in the first place. Bullock's Oriole is known to winter in these same neighborhoods and is often seen at the feeders.

Greater Scaup. These ducks join the assortment of park ducks and quickly become tame, allowing close approaches for photos.

92: Russ Pitman Park and Nature Discovery Center

Migrations, Winter
Free, Daily
Rating: 2
Take Fannin S and Holcombe W (which becomes Bellaire) to Newcastle;

Ringed Turtle-Dove, an introduced species, nests occasionally on the property, although outnumbered by the Eurasian Collared-Doves and Mourning and White-winged doves also occurring here. During spring migration twenty or more species of warblers may be present, as may an assortment of vireos, flycatchers, and other songbirds, especially in the pecan trees. Mississippi Kites and Broad-winged Hawks float over the park during their north- and south-bound journeys. Winter flocks that sweep through the park usually contain kinglets, Blue-headed Vireo, and Orange-crowned, Yellow-rumped, and Pine warblers.

Several species of hummingbirds that nest in the western United States and Canada winter commonly on the Upper Texas Coast. Many of these birds become acclimated to hummingbird feeders, returning year after year to the same perches, occasionally chipping excitedly at a homeowner who is slow to hang up the nectar bottles. Locally, the bulk of these western visitors are Rufous Hummingbirds, a colorful species that nests from the California-Oregon border north to southern Alaska. Rufous Hummingbirds aggressively guard most of the park's nectar feeders, protecting their sugar water from all comers. The possible presence of Allen's Hummingbird, very similar but exceedingly rare, and of the

Broad-tailed Hummingbird, quite similar and usually present, makes the park an excellent place to seek and study the less common species.

93: Houston Arboretum and Memorial Park

Spring, Summer
Memorial Park: Free, Daily
Houston Arboretum: Donation, Daily
Rating: 3
From Loop 610 exit at Woodway and go E 0.2 mile; right at the sign for the Houston Arboretum, located in the western portion of Memorial Park. (Avoid Loop 610 at rush hour; it is one of the nation's busiest freeways.)

Memorial Park, including the Houston Arboretum and Nature Center, is a huge multiuse park near the northwestern corner of Loop 610 and just north of the Galleria shopping center. The habitat ranges from benign neglect to strict protection and offers a large assortment of birds, small mammals, reptiles, amphibians, insects, and plants. The Houston Arboretum protects 155 acres of woodland, ponds, and prairie that may be explored on five miles of trails. Its active education program focuses on all aspects of natural history. Wildlife photographers find an endless array of seasonal themes to pursue in the park. The Houston chapter of the

Native Plant Society of Texas is restoring and improving five acres of prairie within the arboretum.

Big parks support big birds, and Memorial Park is no exception. Wood Duck, Red-shouldered Hawk, Barred Owl, and Pileated Woodpecker nest within its confines. All the typical neighborhood birds are present as well as many of those representative of East Texas woodlands, such as Eastern Screech-Owl, Hooded Warbler, Pine Warbler, and less frequently Kentucky Warbler, Brown-headed Nuthatch (now rare), Red-eyed and White-eyed vireos, and many others.

Watch for Mississippi Kites in late August and early September as they soar over Buffalo Bayou to feed on dragonflies.

During winter additional species appear, including American Robin and Hermit Thrush, Gray Catbird (uncommon), Cedar Waxwing, kinglets, Brown Creeper, and various sparrows, especially White-throated Sparrow.

Butterflies are common, and the arboretum pond, complete with observation tower, is an excellent place to study up to twenty species of dragonflies and damselflies, including such

Houston Arboretum and Memorial Park

Golden-winged Skimmer

showy species as Golden-winged and Slaty skimmers, and Banded Pennant.

After visiting the arboretum, return to Woodway and continue toward the east (right). Parking lots along Woodway and various north-south side roads provide access to Memorial Park. Although not the intimate birding experience provided by the arboretum's interior forest, the rest of the park may produce many of the same species—woodpeckers, Brown-headed Nuthatch, and Pine Warbler can occur here. During spring and fall the park provides a haven for innumerable north- and southbound migrants. Continuing eastward, Woodway feeds into Memorial Drive, which leads to White Oak Park and downtown Houston.

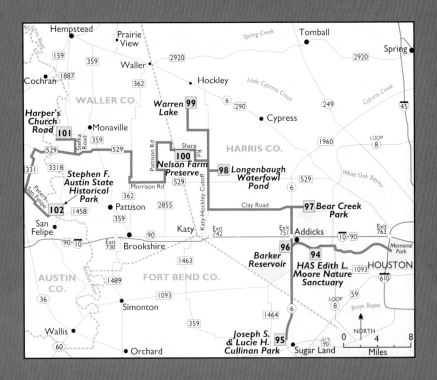

Hempstead Prairie View Tomball Spring

159 359 Waller 2920 Hockley 2920

Cochran 1887 362 6 290 Cypress 249 Cypress Creek 45

WALLER CO. Warren Lake **99** Little Cypress Creek HARRIS CO. 1960 LOOP 8

Harper's Church Road **101** Monaville 359 Sharp Rd **100** Nelson Farm Preserve **98** Longenbaugh Waterfowl Pond 529 White Oak Bayou

Stefka Road Pattison Rd

331 3318 Stephen F. Austin State Historical Park 529 Morrison Rd 529 Clay Road **97** Bear Creek Park

Peters-San Felipe **102** 362 2855 Exit 751 Addicks 10-90 Exit 763

1458 Pattison 359 Katy Exit 742 **96** Memorial Park

San Felipe 90 Brookshire Exit 730 Barker Reservoir **94** 1093 HOUSTON

90 10 1463 HAS Edith L. Moore Nature Sanctuary 610

AUSTIN CO. 1489 FORT BEND CO. 59 LOOP 8

36 Brazos River 1093 Simonton 6 Brays Bayou

1464 359 NORTH

Wallis Joseph S. & Lucie H. Cullinan Park **95** 0 4 8

60 Orchard Sugar Land ALT 90 Miles

Katy Prairie Loop

To the west of Houston, between the Brazos River and the forests to the north, lies the Katy Prairie. Once an endless grassland that echoed with the drummed tattoos of Attwater's Prairie-Chicken and the pounding hooves of vast bison herds, the prairie has been reduced by 130 years of agriculture and development to a patchwork of wet and dry habitats protected by nature preserves and hunting leases or simply by benevolent neglect. Less than 1 percent of the original Texas-Louisiana coastal prairies remains, making them one of our most endangered ecosystems. Of the last 250,000 acres, about a third are now cultivated. The entire area is threatened by introduced vegetation, and commercial and residential development have accelerated due to a decline in rice cultivation and associated land use practices on the Katy Prairie.

Conservation agencies and groups are using various tools to hold onto the pieces of coastal prairie that remain. Among these are land purchases and donations, conservation easements voluntarily limiting development, land management for wildlife values, stewardship for mitigation lands obtained as a result of developer compliance with the Clean Water Act, and the creation and enhancement of prairies through the Houston Area Seed Bank Project.

Nature hangs on as best it can, and the Katy Prairie's major habitats support more than two hundred species of birds. The habitats include grasslands maintained by fire, drought, and grazing; moisture-retaining wetlands that continue to provide for the millions of migratory waterfowl that visit annually; and riparian woodlands following the creek channels that traverse the prairie. Although birding here is good year-round, and each season brings its own coterie of watchable birdlife, in many respects winter is best of all.

During this season the prairie, particularly on clear, windless days, is awash with raptors. An experienced Texas hawk watcher once said: "Learn the red-tail. The others will take care of themselves." The diversity among Red-tailed Hawks—our country's most variable buteo—is enough to hold the keen observer utterly rapt. The Katy Prairie is one of the few venues where birders can see variants that include Eastern, Western, Fuertes', Krider's, Western light morph, Western dark morph, Western Rufous, and Harlan's, all within a few square miles. A smattering of Ferruginous Hawks occurs here every year, and the addition of many other species—Bald Eagle, Prairie Falcon, Peregrine Falcon, Crested Caracara, and White-tailed Hawk—make this one of the state's best venues for wintertime hawk watching.

Open fields host Long-billed Curlew and rarely Mountain Plover as well. Huge blackbird flocks give the patient observer unlimited opportunities to scan for Brewer's Blackbird among the cowbirds, Red-winged Blackbirds, and Common Grackles. Creekside thickets host large winter flocks of Yellow-rumped Warbler, Eastern Bluebird, Carolina Chickadee, and Northern Cardinal, and springtime can turn these same woodlands into migrant passerine bonanzas. Profusions of yaupon holly along the roadsides provide limitless fodder for large and diverse sparrow flocks. Ponds and marshy fields invite concentrations of ducks; ten to fifteen Cinnamon Teal can be seen on a single pond, and thousand-strong congregations of Long-billed Dowitchers peck away in the mud. Avocet, yellowlegs, and countless Killdeer occur here as well. Wet riparian bottomlands along theBrazos can produce Rusty Black-

RAB/Naturewide Images

Red-tailed Hawk

bird, and warmer winters can provide surprises like Yellow-breasted Chat.

The Katy Prairie is particularly accessible to birders in Central Texas—a two-hour drive can put visitors smack in the middle of what may be the coastal region's best winter birding venue. Given the area's fame as a destination for duck and goose hunters, it is particularly important that birders keep off private property. If in any doubt whatsoever, stay off—trespass laws are strictly enforced by game wardens, sheriffs, and property owners. Virtually all public areas will invite entry. All other property should not be entered. Moreover, during hunting season even the innocent act of gazing at ducks on a pond can arouse suspicion. Do not try to get a closer look or a better vantage point by entering private property. Local residents are familiar with birders, so take pains to chat with anyone who slows down to check you out.

Numbers of hedgerow sparrows concentrate here in winter. To see Harris's, White-crowned, and White-throated sparrows, bird the hedgerows. Of particular interest are those that have large stands of fruiting yaupon. Working this hedge habitat and checking each member of the sparrow flock is the best way to find Harris's Sparrow.

94: Houston Audubon Society Edith L. Moore Nature Sanctuary

All Seasons
Free, Daily
Rating: 2
From Memorial Park take Woodway W to Loop 610 N feeder road, stay in left lane 0.5 miles; bear left under Loop 610 to follow left lane fork; Memorial Drive 9.2 miles; left at Wilchester 0.1 mile, sanctuary at second driveway on left.

RAB/Naturewide Images

Wood Ducks

The Houston Audubon Society headquarters and its 17.5 acres represent one of the city's largest protected urban woodlands west of Memorial Park. The site houses a historic log cabin and a modern office building serving the society's 4,200 Audubon members. Most of the property is wooded. Rummel Creek flows through it and can be attractive, though its floodwaters tend to deposit streamside trash with each high water event. Volunteers periodically clean refuse from the creek banks and overhanging vegetation.

Wood Ducks are often seen along the creek, and migrants regularly come to bathe at the pools. The size of the sanctuary, the presence of feeders, the creek, and an attractive pond all serve to enhance species diversity. Winter flocks usually contain Pine Warbler, which may come to the feeders, as well as Yellow-bellied Sapsucker and numerous Yellow-rumped Warblers. Pileated, Red-bellied, and Downy woodpeckers all occur here. Evening prowls often produce a screech-owl. The pond is home to turtles, frogs, snakes, and a nice assortment of dragonflies. There are various children's activities and, with prior notice, docents are available for class visits. During spring migration, the sanctuary can be seething with songbirds, especially during or just after rainy days or cold fronts. The sanctuary is open every day of the year. Call (713) 932-1639 for current hours of operation.

95: Joseph S. and Lucie H. Cullinan Park

All Seasons
Free, Daily
Rating: 2
From I-10 take TX 6 S to the Joseph S. and Lucie H. Cullinan Park, on west side of TX 6 before US 90 in Sugar Land.

Cullinan Park contains weedy fields, scrub, low woodland with some introduced vegetation, and an attractive lake. Boardwalks over the water and a viewing tower attract birders and photographers. Away from the board-

Field Sparrow

walks, access to the water's edge is limited. The observation platform at the end of the boardwalk offers an excellent view of the surrounding lake. In recent years Masked Ducks have wintered in the shallow waters along the boardwalk. During spring and summer listen for Pileated Woodpecker and Yellow-throated Vireo in the swampy forest, Indigo Bunting along the thicket edge, and Dickcissel in the weedy fields. Mississippi Kites soar over the woods, and Loggerhead Shrikes terrorize anole lizards around the picnic tables.

After a devastating drought that shriveled thousands of acres, farmland around Sugarland began changing to residential and commercial property. The importance of Cullinan Park as a habitat island is increasing as the town's strip centers and housing developments spread northward along Highway 6 and Oyster Creek.

Summer birding produces a variety of both landbirds and waterbirds, including Anhinga, Yellow-crowned Night-Heron, Purple Gallinule, Mississippi Kite, Red-shouldered Hawk, Pileated Woodpecker, Yellow-throated Vireo, and Indigo Bunting. During winter, Eastern Phoebe and flocks of Orange-crowned Warbler, Pine Warbler, kinglets, Blue-headed Vireo, and Downy Woodpecker all occur here. Work the scrubby edges for Field, White-crowned, and Harris's sparrows. Wood Ducks, Ring-necked Ducks, a variety of puddle ducks, and a few herons winter on the lake.

Butterflies and dragonflies are common from late spring through fall. Dragonflies include the richly patterned, butterfly-like Halloween Pennant. In weedy fields watch for the dashing black and white Widow Skimmer, a widespread dragonfly that is decidedly scarce around Houston. The most common dragonfly is the Eastern Pondhawk, adult males of which have a pale blue body and green face. Females and young males have a black, green, and white body.

At the edge of the woods just west of the parking lot entrance, watch for a nearly waist-high reddish mound of soil heaped up around several trees. This is a nest of leaf-cutter ants, tropical insects near the northern margin

RAB/Naturewide Images

Halloween Pennant

of their distribution. Among tropical biologists, leaf-cutters are well known and often cited for their important role in cycling nutrients from the forest canopy to the forest floor. In tunnels beneath these mounds, hundreds of thousands of leaf-cutters—sometimes called parasol ants due to the umbrella-like sections of leaf they carry—cultivate a food crop of fungus on chewed leaves from the surrounding woodlands.

Step in close (the ants are harmless), and watch for a few minutes. Worker ants soon emerge from tunnels, where they discard pellets of soil and spent growth medium that rapidly form volcano-like cones, adding to the size of the nest mound. Around the nest, pathways cleared by the ants through the grass and underbrush are also visible.

96: Barker Reservoir

All Seasons
Free, Daily
Rating: 2
From I-10 TX 6 S to Briar Forest, park on west side of TX 6 for Barker Reservoir. Access for Nobel Trail and Barker Lake is here. On TX 6 at Great Texas Coastal Birding Trail sign over Buffalo Bayou, park on the west side and walk to the dike to view flooded wetlands and forest. Reservoir may be entered by a road crossing the levee.

Barker Reservoir was created to control the waters of Buffalo Bayou during periods of high runoff. The reservoir is large, straddling the Fort Bend–Harris County line, and has a capacity of 135,800 acre-feet. To the west of the reservoir, Buffalo Bayou arises from the junction of two smaller streams near Katy. It flows through the reservoir, where its channel is surrounded largely by forest, and then passes newly developed residential areas into Houston. West of the dam are several permanent bodies of water, including Barker Lake at the southern parking entrance on Highway 6. Large expanses of woodlands, their understory dotted with a variety of ponds and shallow depressions, surround these lakes and provide habitat for many forest birds and waterbirds. During all but the highest water events, attractive trails provide birders, hikers, and photographers with access to these woodlands.

Large waders are present all year. During summer most of the region's herons and egrets can be seen here. Birds of prey such as Red-shouldered Hawk and White-tailed Kite are resident. During winter Red-tailed Hawk, Northern Harrier, American Kestrel, Cooper's Hawk, Bald Eagle, Merlin, and Peregrine Falcon are possible. Black-necked Stilts nest along channel margins, although most disappear in fall. A variety of ducks may be present, depending on season and water levels. The more isolated wooded ponds should be checked for Wood Duck and Hooded Merganser.

During winter watch for Rusty Blackbird in Barker Reservoir's mucky or shallowly flooded forest. These birds tend to flock with Red-winged Blackbirds, now and then venturing into the open. One of our least frequently seen members of the blackbird and oriole family, this species occurs occasionally at Barker and at nearby Bear Creek Park but is known at few other local sites. Winter birds have rufous caps and are heavily scaled with rust, the females more so than the males. During summer

the males become glossy black and resemble Brewer's Blackbirds, with which they share the genus *Euphagus*.

Unlike Brewer's Blackbird, the female Rusty Blackbird has a yellow eye throughout the year, but confusion between the two species is unlikely because the female Brewer's tends to be dull gray. Wintering Brewer's Blackbirds are usually found in open fields, a habitat preference that helps birders distinguish them from Rusty Blackbirds.

97: Bear Creek Park

All Seasons
Free, Daily
Rating: 2
From I-10 take TX 6 N; Clay Road E
0.9 mile to Bear Creek Park.

The mature pine-oak woodlands along Bear Creek are home to a number of eastern woodland birds, many near their western limits. Pine Warbler, Swainson's Warbler, Kentucky Warbler, and Hooded Warbler breed here. Golden-crowned Kinglet, which is not always easy to see on the coast, usually winters here with Ruby-crowned Kinglet, Orange-crowned Warbler, and Carolina Chickadee. Eastern Bluebird and Chipping Sparrow are among the winter species that congregate around the parking lots near the entrance. These birds

TLE

Peregrine Falcon

RAB/Naturewide Images

Golden-crowned Kinglet

in turn attract a variety of raptors, including Merlin, Cooper's Hawk, and Sharp-shinned Hawk. The surrounding golf course and open areas host larger birds of prey, including Red-tailed Hawk, Swainson's Hawk, Northern Harrier, and Barn Owl. Pay attention to scolding Blue Jays, which can indicate the presence of a Red-shouldered Hawk or owl. This park can also host an excellent selection of woodpeckers. With luck winter visitors can find Red-headed, Downy, Red-bellied, and Pileated woodpeckers, Northern Flicker, and Yellow-bellied Sapsucker.

TLE

Palm Warbler

FINDING PALM WARBLERS

The western Palm Warbler is drab gray-green in winter, accented with a blush of yellow near the tail. The eastern Palm Warbler in winter retains a distinctive yellow cast and is therefore normally separable from western, and the two geographical populations may be distinguished in the field. The Katy Prairie has both varieties in winter. Habitat specific, they are normally found only in huisache groves and adjacent brush. Western Katy Prairie sites with scrubby stands are best for this bird.

American Woodcock

Rick and Nora Bowers/KAC Productions

FINDING AMERICAN WOODCOCKS

Thirty-six species of regularly occurring shorebirds can be encountered during a spring day on the Upper Texas Coast. All of these may be found by examining the beaches, mudflats, flooded rice fields, rocky jetties, bay islands, ditches, and pond margins along the coast. Most birders will miss the thirty-seventh local shorebird and one of the few that actually nests in East Texas: the American Woodcock. In winter it is usually present in the Houston Arboretum (site 93), and a dusk foray may be rewarded with a glimpse of one hurtling downward through the canopy as it utters its nighthawk-like *peent* call.

This sometimes inept migrant can wind up in people's backyards during fall. A more reliable method for finding it, however, is to visit any woodland on the Katy Prairie that borders a grassy area. By day the American Woodcock remains in the forested wet leaf litter, often flying out into the fields at night. Simply stand at the edge of the right habitat in the evening and watch. Forested habitat along Cypress Creek and Bear Creek is good for finding these birds. They can often be heard when aloft, because when they fly a slot in the wings makes a whistling sound—part of the male's breeding display.

TLE

Vesper Sparrow

98:Longenbaugh Waterfowl Pond

Winter, Migrations
Free, Daily
Rating: 2
From Bear Creek Park (site 97) take
Clay Road W 10.7 miles; Katy-Hock-
ley Cutoff N 4.0 miles to Longen-
baugh Road and the waterfowl pond.

Longenbaugh Waterfowl Pond has
been established by hunting guides
as a refuge for ducks and geese. The
concentration of dabblers here in
winter can reach staggering pro-
portions. At shallow edges look for
Long-billed Dowitcher, yellowlegs,
Least Sandpiper, and lingering Stilt
Sandpiper. Bald Eagles follow the waterfowl to this area, scavenging geese

weakened by disease or crippled by
hunters, and it is not unusual to see
several eagles during a winter's day
afield. Winter can produce excellent sparrow tallies that include Le
Conte's, Vesper, Swamp, and Harris's.
The numbers and diversity of wintering raptors in these fields are often
remarkable. Virtually all the common
races and forms of both eastern and
western Red-tailed Hawk occur, including Harlan's. Northern Harriers
and American Kestrels are abundant;
Peregrine Falcon, Merlin, Sharp-
shinned Hawk, Cooper's Hawk,
Crested Caracara, and White-tailed
Hawk are regulars here.

Plowed rice fields, particularly
those recently flooded, are irresistible
to White Ibis and White-faced Ibis as
well as to flocks of crawfish-eating
Whimbrel. As the water level drops
in spring, waterfowl are replaced by
migrant shorebirds such as American
Golden-Plover, Hudsonian Godwit,
Greater and Lesser yellowlegs, and
Baird's, White-rumped, Pectoral,
and Buff-breasted sandpipers. During summer, look for both species of
whistling-ducks.

To experience the Katy Prairie
requires birding from the roadside.
Remember that these lands are
private, and trespass laws here are
strictly enforced. Game wardens patrol the roads during hunting season,
so please do not trespass under any
circumstances.

99: Warren Lake
Winter
Free, Daily
Rating: 2
Katy-Hockley Cutoff N to Jack Road,
W 1.9 miles, Warren Ranch Road N
1.0 mile. Warren Lake on right.

Bring a scope and do not trespass. Warren Lake may be birded from the road only. After the first October cold fronts, this lake is a major roosting site for geese and a variety of ducks. Sunrise and sunset are especially favorable for birding and for photography, while the geese are arriving and departing. As the flocks pass over, it is usually a simple matter to pick out the smaller Ross's Geese scattered among the Snow Geese. Bald Eagles, Red-tailed Hawks, and Northern Harriers often perch along the lakeshore, ready to take weak or wounded birds. The Common Ground-Dove is often seen along the shoulders of Jack Road. In unfenced areas, especially wet places with rusty-colored bluestem grasses, search for wintering Le Conte's Sparrow, Grasshopper Sparrow, and Sedge Wren.

FINDING GRASSHOPPER SPARROWS

This is the most plastic of the grassland sparrows and occurs in a variety of grassy habitats. Little bluestem, switchgrass, and bush beardgrass attract it. The Grasshopper Sparrow is the only grassland sparrow that is likely to occur within a flock of Savannah Sparrows, so check the often swarming numbers of Savannah Sparrows for this species. Aggressive *pisshing* from the roadside or car window may coax a Grasshopper Sparrow into actually perching on a strand of barbed wire. Note its flat head profile, unstreaked and orange-tinted breast, and pale median crown stripe. During spring and (rarely) summer, listen for its insect-like buzz.

© Jim Morgan

Grasshopper Sparrow

Mound Creek Road, on the opposite side of Warren Lake, can host amazing winter concentrations of Yellow-rumped Warblers, particularly when the yaupon holly trees are feeling the beneficial effects of a particularly wet year and are full of berries.

100: Katy Prairie Conservancy Nelson Farms Preserve

Winter
Free, Daily
Rating: 1
Katy-Hockley Cutoff to Sharp Road, which leads to the preserve. There is a low viewing platform on the south side of the road.

During winter, flocks of geese often roost close to the observation platform. Expect ibis, Great Egret, Snowy Egret,

whistling-ducks, and a few shorebirds, such as Wilson's Snipe and Lesser Yellowlegs. In spring the species diversity increases as more shorebirds appear.

Typically, the hedgerows in this area are alive with wintering sparrows. Among the hordes of White-crowned Sparrows, look for Dark-eyed Junco as well as Lincoln's, Harris's, and (in wetter areas) Swamp sparrows. The densest tangles hold Spotted Towhees and Fox Sparrows, but both can be difficult to see. Sedge Wren may also occur in the grass. During invasion years Lark Bunting occurs in numbers; rarities such as Pyrrhuloxia and Curve-billed Thrasher occur infrequently. The isolated stand of pines adjacent to Nelson Farms Preserve, known among local birders as Barn Owl Woods, may hold a number of interesting winter species such as Red-breasted Nuthatch and Golden-crowned Kinglet. Great Horned Owls and Barn Owls reside in these pines.

101: Harper's Church Road

All Seasons
Free, Daily
Rating: 1
From site 100 take Sharp Road W (it becomes gravel). Take Pattison Road S and Morrison Road E, then FM 2855 S and FM 529 W to Stefka Road N for 1.6 miles; go left on Harper's Church Road.

Spotted Towhee

FINDING LE CONTE'S SPARROWS

This sparrow has the same grass association as Grasshopper Sparrow and normally occurs away from the coast—Katy Prairie (site 100), Attwater National Wildlife Refuge (see details under site 102), and any grassy area with a soggy understory can harbor these birds. However, they also winter in coastal grassland settings such as seacoast bluestem at Galveston Island State Park (site 70) and at Anahuac NWR (sites 49 and 50). The key to seeing Le Conte's Sparrows is to get to the proper habitat, which may include a few small shrubs, and squeak them up. You will never see one otherwise; they simply do not flit about.

© Jim Morgan

Le Conte's Sparrow

Bewick's Wren

species of Bewick's Wren (more rufous above than its western counterpart), and for Lincoln's, Fox, White-throated, and Harris's sparrows. Eastern Bluebirds hunt from the power lines, and the pecan woodlands hold a variety of woodland birds, including woodpeckers, Eastern Phoebe, Blue-headed Vireo, and Yellow-rumped Warbler. During winter the huisache thickets in this area, particularly those around Monaville, host Ladder-backed Woodpecker, which reaches the eastern extent of its range here, as well as Ash-throated Flycatcher, eastern Bewick's Wren, eastern and western forms of Palm Warbler, and Orange-crowned Warbler.

102: Stephen F. Austin State Historical Park (now State Park)

Migrations, Winter
Site fee, Daily
Rating: 2
Harper's Church Road to FM 529 W for 4.7 miles; FM 331 S to birding trail sign. Left on Peters San Felipe Road 4.8 miles, left on Peach Street 0.1 mile; left at fork into park.

At the headquarters pick up a park map and ask for the new bird checklist. It currently includes about eighty species. Sharp-eyed birders should have little trouble adding a number of spring migrants. Drive the park's

Watch for flocks of Horned Larks, and in winter check the plowed fields for Mountain Plover, a locally rare visitor. In late winter Lapland Longspurs may swarm the rice stubble. Check each eagle in this area; a Golden Eagle appears on occasion.

Harper's Church Road continues west toward the Brazos River, although the road does not go all the way to its banks. Some development is evident, but the bottomland forests along this road offer some of the only woodland birding in the region. *Pissh* and squeak at the thickets for Spotted Towhee, for the declining eastern sub-

FINDING HARRIS'S SPARROWS

This Great Plains bird winters in small numbers as far south as the Upper Texas Coast, which is the tail end of its wintering range. Find the bird by locating feeding flocks of White-crowned Sparrows along hedgerows in the Katy Prairie; locally this is the bird with which Harris's Sparrow associates. It utters a distinctive *peeenk* note and is often heard long before it is seen. Although there are a few coastal records, this species is most likely to be seen inland, rarely occurring away from Katy Prairie–type habitat. While looking for it, check feeding flocks carefully for Lincoln's Sparrow, Field Sparrow, Lark Bunting, Song Sparrow, and rarities such as Pyrrhuloxia.

RAB/Naturewide Images

Harris's Sparrow

TLE

Gray Hairstreak

perimeter and various trailer loops. Close to the Brazos River several trails penetrate the woods and provide views of the river; the Cottonwood Trail begins near the amphitheater. The park's habitat is similar to that found along Harper's Church Road and contains Brazos River bottom-land forest of hackberry, sycamore, pecan, cottonwood, and palmetto. During spring every tree seems to have a singing Northern Parula. The large number of Eastern Bluebird boxes should increase the park's population of these lovely birds.

Insect life deserves attention at this site. A number of county dragonfly records have occurred here. By late February, butterflies become noticeable and freshly emerged Eastern Tiger Swallowtail, American Lady, and Gray Hairstreak are on the wing, followed shortly by Little Wood Satyr and Carolina Satyr.

The Attwater Prairie-Chicken National Wildlife Refuge is just a few miles away; it is not profiled in this book because it is part of the Central Texas Coast portion of the Great Texas Coastal Birding Trail. To proceed there from the Stephen F. Austin park, exit by following the main pavement (yellow lines) just over half a mile; take FM 1458 south (left) for two miles, Interstate 10 west three miles, Texas Highway 36 south one mile, and then FM 3013 west to the refuge.

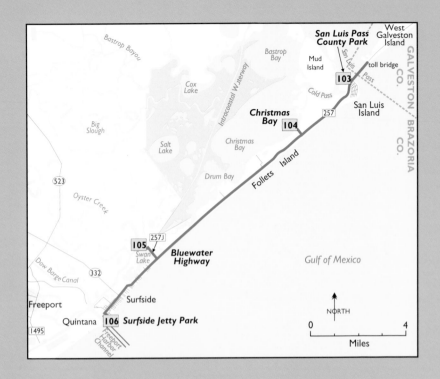

Bastrop Bayou

Bastrop Bay

San Luis Pass County Park

West Galveston Island

Mud Island

toll bridge

103

Cox Lake

Intracoastal Waterway

Cold Pass

San Luis Island

San Luis Island

Christmas Bay

104

257

Big Slough

Salt Lake

Christmas Bay

Follets Island

GALVESTON CO.

523

Drum Bay

BRAZORIA CO.

Oyster Creek

257J

105

Gulf of Mexico

Dow Barge Canal

332

Swan Lake

Bluewater Highway

NORTH

Freeport

Surfside

0   4

Quintana   106 Surfside Jetty Park

Miles

1495

Freeport Harbor Channel

Bluewater Loop

The Bluewater Loop provides a short foray along Follets Island, which separates the Gulf from West Bay, the westernmost portion of Galveston Bay. The island is narrow; both the bay and the Gulf can be seen from most sites along the route. Although sites are close together, this loop is attractive because it presents significantly different habitats. On the sheltered bay side, fine silts from coastal bayous fall out of suspension and form muddy flats that become vegetated both above and below the water line. Shorebirds probe for the worms, clams, crabs, and shrimp that burrow into these rich sediments, and herons fish in the more open pools. At several sites, channels dredged through the mucky bottom allow those with canoes or kayaks to launch into the bay.

In contrast to the bay side, the Gulf's pale sands sparkle just across the road, where Sanderlings chase waves back and forth, picking tiny amphipod crustaceans from the soupy sand at the water's edge. After a storm the beach may be festooned with souvenirs of the open seas, including jellyfish, sargassum weed, Portuguese man-o-war, purple *Janthina* snails, by-the-wind sailors, and bottles encrusted with goose-neck barnacles. The Gulf's beaches are a popular area for up to ten species of gulls and terns and several kinds of shorebirds. The beach flocks change with the seasons. Black Terns, although hard to find in April, become regular here from May and are common in summer and fall. Along with the Least Tern, they can easily be found among the beach flocks. Winter can be good for Bonaparte's Gull, which arrives in mid-December, and always check for rarities such as Lesser Black-backed Gull. The Sandwich Tern is most common from spring through fall.

Despite the popularity of these beaches, during much of the year they are not crowded. After the relative congestion of High Island and Galveston, this loop invites visitors into a calmer, more relaxed frame of mind.

103: San Luis Pass County Park

All Seasons
Site fee, Daily
Rating: 1
From West Galveston Island, cross toll bridge over San Luis Pass. Coastal highway becomes County Road 257. After bridge exit right to park.

This spot offers another view of the extensive flats at San Luis Pass. Watch for white and pied individuals of Reddish Egret, as they seem more common here than at Bolivar Flats. During spring and summer the large yellow blossoms of beach evening primrose grow at the higher parts of the beach and amid concrete rubble. This coastal specialty has blossoms that are often more than three inches across. Although numerous varieties of yellow primrose are found in inland Texas, this species' range is restricted to the sandy continental margin on islands, dunes, and marsh edge, and it rarely occurs more than a few yards inland.

Leaving the park vicinity, continue westward and check the grassy areas for Long-billed Curlew, which feeds in the freshwater marshes. The Short-eared Owl can occur in irruptive years but is a rarity. Sedge Wrens winter commonly here, and White-tailed Kites are often numerous along this stretch of road, nesting in the tall shrubs. A number of signed spots provide public access to the beach. These beaches, popular with anglers, are usually hard packed and safe to drive. Watch for Red Knot and Black-bellied Plover among the common Willets and Sanderlings. Slowly approach the flocks of roosting gulls and terns and sort out the species, watching for Common Terns among the Forster's Terns, and for hundreds of Sandwich

RAB/Naturewide Images

Black Terns (nonbreeding plumage)

FINDING GULLS AND TERNS

Unlike the cryptic and secretive grassland sparrows, which live their lives under the strictest secrecy, gulls and terns are easily found throughout most coastal areas. The chief difficulty in finding these birds lies not so much in locating as in locating particular species. The key to finding certain target gulls and terns is tied to seasonality. The Black Tern and Gull-billed Tern, for example, occur from spring through fall and must be looked for during this seasonal window. Although large flocks of gulls and terns on an exposed mudflat may appear conspicuous, differentiating between species when birds are tightly packed together invites another important strategic angle—that of the slow, deliberate scan with a scope. Look carefully at each member in a flock to determine which species are present.

RAB/Naturewide Images

Bolivar Flats

Terns sandwiched among the Royal Terns. The disparate age groups provide good opportunities to look at the various plumages and leg colors as the young birds mature.

Check the salt marshes for a good variety of big waders such as Roseate Spoonbill and Tricolored Heron.

Laughing Gulls predominate in summer, and in spring look for Ring-billed and Herring gulls, Royal, Caspian, and Forster's terns, and a few Common Terns. Visitors from other parts of the country may be amused to see territorial Willets standing on power lines on Follets Island. Snowy and

Piping plovers occur here most of the year except during the middle of summer. In the fall and summer large numbers of Least and Black terns occur as well.

104: Christmas Bay

All Seasons
Free, Daily
Rating: 1
Brazoria County Road 257 S to Christmas Bay and the Christmas Bay Scenic View.

Galveston Bay and its sister bays once were vegetated with extensive beds of subtidal sea grasses. When John James Audubon visited the Texas coast in 1837, he commented that the Tundra Swan, a sea grass grazer with a long neck that aids in foraging, was one of the common waterfowl on Galveston Bay. This once common bird would now constitute a very rare sighting were it to occur here. Christmas Bay is the last basin in the Galveston Bay complex to retain significant sea grass beds. Along all sections of the Bluewater Loop watch the *Spartina* marsh, which is excellent habitat for Seaside Sparrow and Clapper Rail.

105: Bluewater Highway

All Seasons
Free, Daily
Rating: 1
Just west of the site 105 birding trail sign, County Road 257J goes to the bay and a Brazoria County public boat ramp.

Check the flats along County Road 257J for nesting Wilson's Plover and other shorebirds. Wilson's Plovers eat fiddler crabs that live in countless numbers near the margin of the open mudflats and the extensive stands of pickleweed. Pools near the boat ramp harbor larger waders and a few shorebirds. Keep an eye out for

Wilson's Plover

FINDING NORTHERN GANNETS

This bird feeds in clear offshore waters. Where the Gulf is muddy, you will not find Northern Gannet. As you drive the coastline between High Island and the Bolivar ferry or follow any open stretch of road on the Bluewater Loop, scan the Gulf for color. There are days when the brown water suddenly ends, and beyond it the sea is deep blue. This "bluewater line" demarcates the sediment-filled longshore current, and it is along this blue-brown boundary that the Northern Gannet most often occurs. Large movements off Bolivar sometimes include hundreds of individuals. A wintering Texas bird, it can also be seen in the blue water off the Surfside and Quintana jetties.

white morph Reddish Egrets among the Snowy and Great egrets. To find a white Reddish Egret, watch for its bicolored pink and black bill and shaggy neck feathering. Its drunken, staggering feeding behavior usually allows identification even at a great distance.

Just beyond the CR 257J turnoff, note the Stahlman Nature Park and Beach Pavilion, a Surfside Beach recreational area. There are open and shaded sites at the pavilion, bathrooms, an outdoor shower, and beach access. The crabbing pier across the road is seasonally interesting for waders and good for Clapper Rail as well. The tamer waders can easily be photographed, with walk-up Tricolored Heron a distinct possibility. Close looks at the nearshore birdlife can be had as the birds feed on small blue crabs, mullet, and killifish.

Go southwest on Bluewater Highway ten miles to Texas Highway 332 in Surfside and note the large bridge on the right. The bay margin is limited here because of development but may be reached for additional birding by driving the access roads below the bridge.

106: Surfside Jetty Park

Winter
Free, Daily
Rating: 1
From County Road 257, take TX 332 W 1.0 mile; Parkview Road S 0.2 mile to park.

Enter the park and pay the entrance fee, or drive past the turn to the park and follow the road just a bit farther to the jetty, where there is a beach

RAB./Naturewide Images

Willet

with parking and public access. Playground equipment here makes this a good stop for birders traveling with nonbirding youngsters. Necessities can be obtained from the small store. The jetty now offers better footing than it once did.

Purple Sandpiper, seen here a handful of times, may be absent for a decade or more. When this bird occurs, it constitutes a significant sighting. Carefully inspect any Dunlin-like birds that are roosting or feeding on the rocks if you are intent on searching

for this locally rare arctic breeder. Frigatebirds may occur off the jetty, but they are often seen at great distances and are difficult to spot without careful study. Red-breasted Merganser is regular around the Surfside and Quintana jetties. There is a narrow window in the dead of winter for Bonaparte's Gull. Occasionally, hundreds of Bonaparte's Gulls follow ships into the channel, foraging on marine life stirred up by a huge tanker's propellers or scavenging on small fishes that have been discarded from shrimp boats.

TLE

Loggerhead Shrike

FINDING LOGGERHEAD SHRIKES

Check the trees along the edge of Stahlman Nature Park, where Loggerhead Shrikes can be found with relative ease. They occur throughout the Follets Island and Quintana areas and nest in palms.

Scoters, jaegers, and other rarities have been recorded off these jetties, but their detection requires hours of meticulous scanning with a high-powered scope. Most birders want to spend their time here looking at the abundant and easily seen Willets, Snowy Egrets (sitting right on the railings), Sanderlings, Ruddy Turnstones (on the rocks), Double-crested Cormorants (feeding in the channel and off the jetties), and a good mix of gulls and terns.

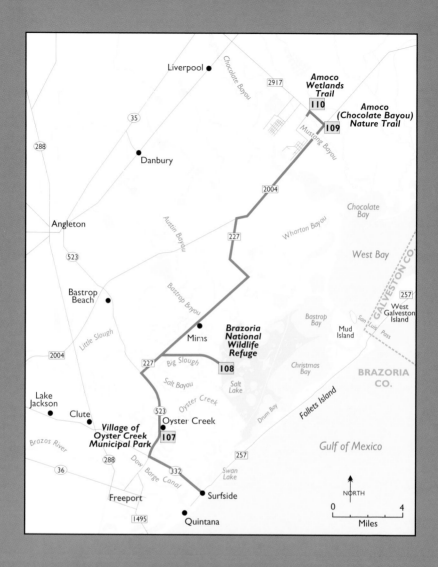

Liverpool

Chocolate Bayou

2917

Amoco
Wetlands
Trail

110

109

Amoco
(Chocolate Bayou)
Nature Trail

35

288

Danbury

Mustang Bayou

2004

Angleton

Austin Bayou

227

Wharton Bayou

Chocolate
Bay

West Bay

523

Bastrop
Beach

Bastrop Bayou

Mims

Brazoria
National
Wildlife
Refuge

Bastrop
Bay

Mud
Island

257

West
Galveston
Island

Little Slough

2004

227

Big Slough

108

Salt Bayou

Oyster Creek

Christmas
Bay

Salt
Lake

Follets Island

BRAZORIA
CO.

Lake
Jackson

Clute

Village of
Oyster Creek
Municipal Park

523

Oyster Creek

107

Drum Bay

Brazos River

Gulf of Mexico

36

288

Dow Barge Canal

332

257

Swan
Lake

NORTH

0   4

Freeport

Surfside

Miles

1495

Quintana

Coastal Plains Loop

This is a small loop with five sites, the final three of which have various access issues. All are located in low-lying Brazoria County. Five of the sites offer water access, and the last is likely to be seasonally flooded. All of these sites were once part of the aboriginal coastal tall grass prairie that stretched from central Louisiana to southeast Texas. At several coastal refuges, controlled burns are utilized to clear brush and enhance prairie grasses, in much the same way that coastal cattle ranchers burn their fields to provide new growth for their livestock. These prairies can be spectacular for wildflowers. A drab winter vista may be a riot of color during spring and summer. Be sure to carry a guide to Texas wildflowers.

In spring and fall migration, during or just after a cold front or rain, be certain to check the Village of Oyster Creek Municipal Park, one of the better birding woodlands on the coast. This park has tall, older trees not present along most of the loop and is therefore more attractive to tired migrants.

The centerpiece of this loop is the Brazoria National Wildlife Refuge, and a morning or a day spent here during summer, winter, or migrations provides an excellent selection of coastal birds. Trails, boardwalks, gardens, informational pamphlets, parking spots, picnic tables, guided walks, and other visitor amenities further enhance a visit to the Brazoria refuge.

107: Village of Oyster Creek Municipal Park

Migrations
Free, Daily
Rating: 1
From Surfside, TX 332 W 3.7 miles; FM 523 N 2.4 miles to park.

This wooded park is beautiful and perfectly situated to attract migrating songbirds searching for trees along the coast's boggy fringes. The spreading live oaks and hackberries neither crowd together nor create overly tall canopies, a combination that yields perfect viewing conditions. During winter, mixed flocks that usually

Rick Snowden

Carolina Chickadee

include several species of woodpeckers respond vigorously to *pisshing*.
The Rusty Blackbird is rare here; it is
always worthwhile, though, to look
carefully at blackbird flocks that forage in wet areas along the boundary
fence. A Red-shouldered Hawk often
perches on the power poles around
the parking area; look too for Osprey
overhead.

Stand on the pier and look down
into the shallow water. The creek
is brackish, and the oysters, fiddler
crabs, and jumping mullet are on
loan from the Gulf. These estuarine
species, living in coastal sites where

salt water and fresh water mix, take
advantage of the mix of rich nutrients
found here. The dense soup of plankton, beds of sea grasses, and huge
populations of mud-dwelling invertebrates attract herons, egrets, gulls,
terns, and dozens of shorebirds to eat
the fish, crustaceans, and mollusks.

This pleasant site has nice play-
grounds but can require maximal
applications of mosquito repellent.
The canopy is lovely, but the best
way to find birds here is by checking
the area where the canopy's edge
transitions to understory on private
land (marked by a chain-link fence).

In migration, birds occur in the live oak canopy but also within this edge habitat, which should not be neglected. Walk the fenceline to see the maximum number of birds. Birders enjoy the antics of titmice and chickadees here, and the woodland edge sections can be highly productive during migrations. Kingfishers work the fishing pier, and raptors such as Red-shouldered Hawk and Osprey occur as well. This is a good site for most of the common woodland birds because it connects with the contiguous woodland along Oyster Creek.

108: Brazoria National Wildlife Refuge

All Seasons
Free, Dawn to Dusk
Rating: 3
From Oyster Creek Municipal Park, FM 523 N 2.6 miles; County Road 227 E 1.8 miles to the refuge.

During winter, especially December and January, the refuge protects large numbers of wintering waterfowl: some 30,000–50,000 Snow, White-fronted, Ross's and Canada geese, and upwards of 30,000 puddle ducks. These large concentrations, however, cannot be seen from the tour loop. Landbirds are abundant during winter and summer, and nesting waterbirds include coastal specialties such as Gull-billed Tern, Roseate Spoonbill, and Seaside Sparrow. If the water levels are suitable, Purple Gallinule can be seen at the sign-in area. The 7.5-mile tour route leads visitors to most of the refuge habitats and is sprinkled with picnic tables placed adjacent to pond edges, making them ideal for snackers and photographers.

The nature trail behind the pavilion begins as a marsh boardwalk crossing Big Slough, then penetrates trees and brush that are attractive to both wintering and migrant songbirds. Vermilion Flycatcher occurs consistently here in some years. Continue on the tour route to Olney Pond, which is often seething with puddle ducks, ibis, shorebirds, and wintering geese. There is a lone record

RAB/Naturewide Images

Vermilion Flycatcher

here for Trumpeter Swan. Numerous alligators live on the refuge and are generally visible at the pond margins. The left side of Cross Trails Marsh, just beyond Olney Pond, is good for freshwater birds such as ibis, puddle ducks, and shorebirds. On the right, brackish water attracts good numbers of saltwater shorebirds, egrets, and a few Black Skimmers from the nearby colony. Seaside Sparrows can be brought up to the edge of the marsh grass by squeaking or *pishing,* and this is one of the better coastal spots to see this bird, particularly if the tide is out. Follow the refuge map to the turnaround and scan for waterbirds at Roger's Pond. During summer, check the muddy or sandy openings in the marsh for nesting Black-necked Stilt and Gull-billed Tern.

An observation platform about a quarter mile from Teal Pond provides long prairie views where wintering geese and Sandhill Cranes and nesting White-tailed Kites can all be seen at a distance.

Teal Pond itself attracts dabblers and divers in winter, including Bufflehead, scaup, and Redhead; it is the best spot for diving ducks on the tour loop. In summer check for Black-necked Stilt; Wilson's Plover is regular but in sparse numbers. During summer this is one of the best freshwater shorebird spots on the Upper Texas Coast and should be checked at all costs. The pond creates a prairie pothole effect because of its shallow grade. When dry summer weather causes the muddy edges to appear, the deepest part of the pond is only six to ten inches in depth. This expansive, shallow pond with muddy margins goes dry in July–August, and as the pond dries up it attracts thousands of shorebirds that feast on the exposed food sources. Twenty shorebird species can occur here, and the pond constitutes an incredible wildlife spectacle when it is popping with birds.

The row of salt cedars that come up to the viewing platform can trap good numbers of migrants, as it is the only place for migrating birds to land. Nelson's Sharp-tailed Sparrow has been seen from the platform. The fields are best for wintering sparrows—Savannah with an occasional Vesper Sparrow in migration. Find Le Conte's Sparrow by walking through the grass. A wide variety of sparrows can occur here, so check every little brown bird that pops up. On the return, go back through the gate and retrace the entrance road for about two miles through the coastal prairie, which is good for Eastern Meadowlark and White-tailed Kite, prairie birds, and more sparrows. This is one of the best coastal sites for White-tailed Hawk; due to the lack of suitable perches, they have to be up and flying in order to be seen.

Variegated Fritillary

RAB/Naturewide Images

109: Amoco (Chocolate Bayou) Nature Trail

Bayou corridors can offer good birding during migrant fallout weather because there is so little other suitable passerine habitat. This small bayou with vegetation is great cover for tired migrants, but questionable or difficult access makes it unrecommended to birders.

110: Amoco Wetlands Trail

Not recommended.

111: Site removed from trail

Ash-throated Flycatcher

FINDING FLYCATCHERS

The Empidonax *Flycatchers*: The variety within this genus is best represented during fall migration. With the exception of Acadian Flycatchers, which breed along the coast, most arrive in late spring and migrate through over a very short stretch of time in May, making them difficult to spot. Fall migration, however, begins early. These flycatchers arrive in summer, peak from mid-August through Labor Day, and can remain through the end of the year, with the odd Least Flycatcher or two staying through December. Use the period from mid- to late summer as the season to look for *Empidonax.*

The *Empidonax* flycatchers are more commonly seen in the fall because in spring their migration is tightly timed along an isotherm. They are not moving north until the weather is warm enough to produce bugs, and by the time it has grown warm enough, they must move through quickly in order to breed and nest. Thus the spring period during which they can be common is very short. In fall these birds linger because Texas is warm and buggy. Least and Yellow-bellied flycatchers do not go beyond Mexico and can afford to tarry.

With some of the *Empidonax,* vocalizations are the only way to make a positive identification. Many birders are happy simply to note a gray-green flycatcher with a white eyering and call it an *Empidonax.* Those

Eastern Kingbird

TLE

who want a finer level of detail need to become familiar with vocalizations in order to identify the bird. *Empidonax* sometimes respond to Eastern Screech-Owl calls, both by appearing and by calling.

Least and Yellow-bellied flycatchers are common fall migrants. Least Flycatcher is a scrub bird and prefers rattlebean and thorn-scrub habitat. It rarely gets more than a few feet off the ground and can be found around salt cedar and woodland edge. Yellow-bellied Flycatcher is often seen in interior woodlands, especially during the second week of May, and is more often heard than seen. Willow and Alder flycatchers are among the most enigmatic of all Texas birds. Their status is poorly understood. Alder Flycatcher is an uncommon but regular migrant, best identified by its Downy Woodpecker–like call note. Willow Flycatcher is virtually indistinguishable from Alder except by voice, and by the time it reaches Texas it is not particularly vocal.

The Myiarchus *Flycatchers*: Great Crested Flycatcher is the eastern woodland breeder. Brown-crested Flycatcher is a South Texas resident currently pushing its way north, occurring at coastal woodlands such as Brazoria NWR and Galveston Island State Park (sites 108 and 70), and woodlands near Freeport. It is a rare migrant and winter resident on the Upper Texas Coast. Ash-throated Flycatcher is a regular wintering bird and should be searched for in weedy scrub habitat and huisache stands found in Fort Bend, Colorado, and Waller counties. This is an open scrub bird and is rarely seen during migration on the coast.

Kingbirds: Eastern, Western, and Couch's kingbirds are all found in west Harris County. Look for Eastern Kingbird, a common breeder, along woodland edges, hedgerows, fencerows, scattered trees at Anahuac, marsh edge, and river edge. Large numbers migrate through our area in spring and fall. Western Kingbirds are local but regular breeders in the Houston area, almost exclusively associated with power transfer station transformers and superstructures. They are uncommon but regular spring and fall migrants and prefer open barbed wire fences and telephone lines. Couch's Kingbird is a tropical species that has gradually moved north over the last twenty-five years, and it is increasingly common, though still rare with only a few seen each year. Found in winter on the immediate coast, but inland to Brazoria County and west Harris County as well, this is an exciting bird to see. The Tropical Kingbird, which has become established in southernmost Texas, should become more regular on the Upper Texas Coast. In the field it is most reliably differentiated from Couch's Kingbird by its call—their plumages are extremely similar.

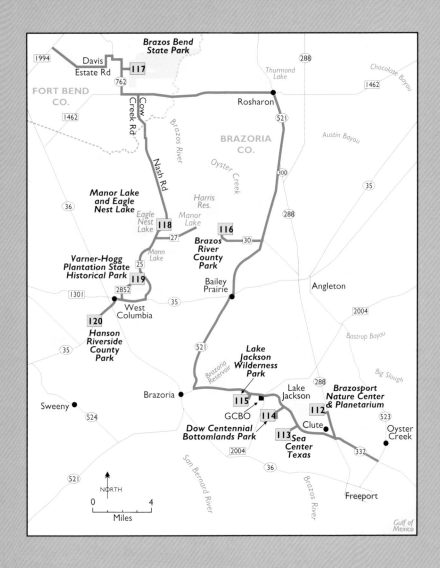

1994

Davis
Estate Rd

117

**Brazos Bend
State Park**

762

Thurmond
Lake

288

1462

Chocolate Bayou

**FORT BEND
CO.**

Cow Creek Rd

Rosharon

521

1462

**BRAZORIA
CO.**

Austin Bayou

35

Nash Rd

Brazos River

Oyster Creek

300

288

36

**Manor Lake
and Eagle
Nest Lake**

Harris
Res.

Eagle
Nest
Lake

Manor
Lake

118

27

116

30

**Brazos
River
County
Park**

**Varner-Hogg
Plantation State
Historical Park**

Mann
Lake

25

119

2852

Bailey
Prairie

Angleton

35

1301

West
Columbia

35

2004

120

**Hanson
Riverside
County
Park**

Bastrop Bayou

35

521

Brazoria Reservoir

**Lake
Jackson
Wilderness
Park**

Big Slough

Sweeny

Brazoria

Lake
Jackson

288

**Brazosport
Nature Center
& Planetarium**

524

115

GCBO

114

112

Clute

523

Oyster
Creek

**Dow Centennial
Bottomlands Park**

113 **Sea
Center
Texas**

332

2004

36

San Bernard River

Brazos River

521

NORTH

0   4

Miles

Freeport

Gulf of
Mexico

Brazoria Loop

The Brazoria Loop contains nine far-flung sites in Brazoria and Fort Bend counties. There is much to see here, so plan to spend at least two days visiting the entire loop. Some of the sites are small and warrant a quick peek first thing in the morning; others can easily consume several hours. Visitors to Brazos Bend State Park can easily spend an entire day watching and photographing the reptiles, amphibians, butterflies, and birds.

The Brazos River bottomland hardwood forests define the ecology of this loop. They provide nesting grounds for neotropical migrants such as Mississippi Kite, Yellow-billed Cuckoo, Acadian and Great Crested flycatchers, Red-eyed, White-eyed, and Yellow-throated vireos, Hooded, Swainson's, and Yellow-throated warblers, Northern Parula, Summer Tanager, and Orchard Oriole. Drive this route on any sunny spring or early summer morning and listen to the variety of birdsongs that issue forth from migrants singing on territory. Much of the surrounding forest along the river has already been cleared, and visitors should note the critical importance of this remaining habitat.

More than a hundred species of butterflies, more than a hundred species of dragonflies and damselflies, numerous reptiles, amphibians, and mammals, and a rich palette of spring and summer wildflowers make this a particularly appealing loop.

112: Brazosport Nature Center and Planetarium (NCAP) Nature Trail

All Seasons
Free, Daily; call (979) 265-7661 for planetarium hours
Rating: 3
From FM 523 and TX 332, take TX 332 W 3.5 miles; Business 288 N 2.9 miles; College Blvd. W 0.2 mile to first entrance, turn right to Brazosport College. Park at Brazosport Center for the Arts and Sciences.

The trail is relatively short and easily walked, and the labeled trees and dense understory make the Brazosport Nature Center trail a worthwhile

Black-throated Blue Warbler

RAB./Naturewide Images

stop, especially during spring migration. During one Migration Celebration birding festival, a locally rare Black-throated Blue Warbler was seen here. American Woodcock, an irregular and hard-to-find bird for this site, has occurred in early August. In winter, at least five species of woodpeckers inhabit these woods, including Pileated Woodpecker. Brown Thrashers and Hermit Thrushes skulk in the understory, and Blue-headed Vireos often join the local insectivore flocks.

113: Sea Center Texas

All Seasons
Free, Closed on Sunday mornings, Mondays, and major holidays; call (979) 292-0100 to confirm hours of operation
Rating: 2
In Lake Jackson, TX 288/332 to Plantation Drive S 0.7 mile to sea center.

Birders interested in marine ecosystems enjoy visiting the saltwater fish hatchery as well as the fresh- and saltwater marshes, boardwalk, and interpretive center. Because of their favorable location, these wetlands attracted scads of shorebirds and her-

Marl Pennant

RAB/Naturewide Images

ons during the bulldozing operations that created the wetlands. Many species of ducks, shorebirds, and large waders regularly use the site. The White Ibis is especially common. Scan the hatchery ponds behind the center, since they attract gulls, kingfishers, and wintering Osprey. Dragonflies are typically numerous in summer, especially the black and yellow Seaside Dragonlet. Marl Pennant, another species associated with mineralized water and decidedly scarce on the coast, should be looked for here. The center and associated boardwalks do not open at daybreak, so plan to stop here later in the morning.

The boardwalk provides excel-lent views of egrets and shorebirds. Ducks have become scarce because of increased foot traffic, but some may still be seen. The aquariums contain many species of native Texas fish and have a "touch tank" for children to learn about crabs and fish. The star of the show is a three-hundred-pound grouper named Gordon.

114: Dow Centennial Bottomlands Park

Migrations, Winter
Free, Daily
Rating: 3
From Sea Center Texas continue on

Scarlet Tanager

TX 332 W 1.2 miles; Oak Drive S 0.5 mile; left on Lake Road and right into Maclean Park.

The Dow Centennial Bottomlands Park is behind the Maclean Park pavilion at 93 Lake Road. A two-mile nature trail, with benches at the end, winds through wooded bottomlands where spring migrants abound. Nearby is the Gulf Coast Bird Observatory. To reach it, return to Texas Highway 332 and go west about 1.3 miles to enter the observatory on the left. This site is just across Buffalo Camp Bayou from Lake Jackson Wilderness Park, so both may be birded together. The observatory is dedicated to coordinating migrant bird research and has

ties with a number of Latin American research and conservation organizations. A half-mile trail runs through the bottomland forest. One fork leads to the Dow Freshwater Canal, the edge of which may be birded. The other winds through the forest and reaches a road that leads back to the observatory. The trail begins at the end of the barbed wire fence near the entrance. Staff members are present during the week until 4:30 P.M. Stop by the office to get information about special birds or events. A map is available, presenting additional information on newly opened birding sites around Lake Jackson. On weekends, park at the gate or in the lot of the Lake Jackson Wilderness Park and walk back to the observatory grounds. The observatory runs a number of field trips, weekend migration and identification workshops, workdays, and other bird-related events. Call (979) 480-0999 or visit the Web site http://www.gcbo.org for a current schedule.

115: Lake Jackson Wilderness Park

Migrations, Winter
Free, Daily
Rating: 1
On TX 332 across Buffalo Camp Bayou from Gulf Coast Bird Observatory (site 114).

Blue-headed Vireo

Because it rarely freezes here, these bottomland woods tend to remain lush throughout the winter. Each year a number of neotropical migrants, birds that would otherwise have continued to the tropical forests of Central and South America, remain in these insect-rich woods. Among the migrant birds watch for lingerers such as Ovenbird, Northern Parula, and Black-and-white and Yellow-throated warblers. This park of almost five hundred acres has an attractive four-mile trail on which to photograph graceful Spanish moss–draped trees, contrasting with the angular palmettos growing in the understory.

Finding birds in these woods can be challenging because the habitat is extensive and the birds are not concentrated. The occasional feeding flock may be encountered, but most birds tend to remain obscured by the canopy. A few wintering warblers can be called up with screech-owl imitations. Pileated Woodpecker, White-eyed Vireo, Wilson's Warbler, and Blue-headed Vireo all occur here.

The lush palmetto habitat is beautiful, and constitutes critical bottomland habitat for migrants to and from Latin America.

116: Brazos River County Park

All Seasons
Free, Daily
Rating: 2
TX 332 W; TX 521 (ramp appears suddenly on right) N 12.0 miles; TX 35/521 E 0.2 mile and bear left on TX 521 E. After 7.1 miles go left on County Road 30 (signed Brazos River County Park, Holiday Lakes) 2.7 miles; turn north into Planter's Point and follow Colony Lane to park gate.

Large waders occur here all year. Check the ponds that abut the roadside for a variety of dragonflies, including such species as Great Pondhawk and Red Saddlebags. Resident Red-shouldered Hawks are quite common, perching on utility wires along the roadside and often protesting loudly at birders who stop for a look.

Enter the park and listen in the splendid live oaks for common species such as Northern Cardinal, Tufted Titmouse, and Carolina Chickadee. Walk the boardwalk along the river, listening for Acadian Flycatcher (spring through early fall), Northern Parula, Summer Tanager, Yellow-billed Cuckoo, White-eyed Vireo, and

RAB/Naturewide Images

Red Saddlebags

FINDING ANHINGAS

In summer this bird is most common in interior marshes and swamps, such as at Brazos Bend State Park (site 117). It migrates through the coastal area in fall, often in significant numbers. Look for large flocks kettling together (forming a rising, swirling group, likened by some to the appearance of boiling water) with Broad-winged Hawks, Wood Storks, and American White Pelicans. Anhingas look like gliders—stiff wings, long tail, and long neck. Find the bird by scanning the snags and stumps upon which they perch while sunning, and check marshy waters for their unique aquatic profile, a mostly submerged body with only the neck and head visible. The Anhinga's long, thin, unhooked bill, tiny head, and buffy neck and breast (female) or white streaked wings (male) differentiate it from superficially similar cormorants.

RAB/Naturewide Images

Anhinga

other songbirds. Swainson's Warbler nests here but can be hard to find because of its skulking ways. Listen for its strident whistling song, the last note or two often being emphasized.

117: Brazos Bend State Park

All Seasons
Site fee, Daily
Rating: 3
FM 521 N to FM 1462; take FM 1462 W 10.9 miles; TX 762 N 1.3 miles; Park Road 72 turns into entrance.

During winter, Bald Eagles, other raptors, geese, and Sandhill Cranes often occur in fields along area roads, so be alert for birds on the way to the park. Approaching the office, watch for white-tailed deer and listen for the chittering of Sedge Wrens (winter and spring) along the weedy entrance road.

Brazos Bend is located in Fort Bend County, about twenty-eight miles south of Houston. The park is a favorite of visitors from out of state, and during a spring trip first-time visitors from the western United States can net a number of species for a life list here. The park covers 4,897 acres of mixed habitats. Its eastern boundary includes 3.2 miles of Brazos River frontage, accessible from a trailhead at Hale Lake.

Bring a telescope. Masked Ducks have intermittently been present in Pilant Lake near the tower. The birds

Brazos Bend State Park

RAB./Naturewide Images

Common Moorhen

were seen during various months, but nesting was not confirmed. This species may recur, so observers should watch the vegetated lake margins closely. In winter colorful and attractive Cinnamon Teal as well as Vermilion Flycatcher occur in the tower area. Early in spring, Great Blue Heron nests are often present close to the tower. A scope allows viewers to enjoy the antics of the adults and young. While watching them from the top deck, or scanning for a rare Least Grebe, visitors may get an eye-level look at a Mississippi Kite, Scissor-tailed Flycatcher, White Ibis, Wood Duck, whistling-duck, Red-shouldered Hawk, or Pileated Woodpecker flying by.

Throughout spring and early summer, a large heronry that includes Roseate Spoonbill and Tricolored Heron is visible through a scope, far across the marsh. Purple Gallinule, Common Moorhen, American Coot, King Rail, and Least Bittern occur here. This is one of the farthest inland locations for Boat-tailed Grackles, which nest in large numbers in the marshes. Prothonotary Warbler and Orchard Oriole sing in the willows along the levee, and Barred Owls call in the evenings. Occasionally these owls may be heard and observed during the day. Visitors who linger for Eastern Screech-Owl can stargaze at the park's observatory. The George Observatory, a branch of

RAB/Naturewide Images

the Houston Museum of Natural Science, is open each Saturday for sun, moon, and star viewing from 3:00 to 10:00 P.M. Special group or class visits may be arranged for other evenings.

For nature photographers Brazos Bend is a source of unending inspiration. Stately yellow lotus blossoms and huge, moss-festooned live oaks provide a variety of subjects, as do the wildflowers, spiders, grasshoppers, dragonflies, and butterflies that occur in profusion. When getting down to inspect something closely, mind the fire ants; they are plentiful and leave memorable wounds. Watch for and avoid their mounds, distinctive piles of loose soil. Some birds may permit a close approach—Red-bellied Woodpecker, Carolina Wren, Swamp Sparrow, Black-bellied Whistling-Duck, White Ibis, American Bittern, Anhinga, Yellow-crowned Night-Heron, and Green, Great Blue, Little Blue, and Tricolored herons—adding to the park's appeal for photographers seeking full-frame images of these attractive birds. Even normally skittish species such as Blue-winged Teal, Pileated Woodpecker, and White-eyed Vireo can be photographed here. The park's frogs, lizards, snakes, turtles, and alligators are plentiful, if not always patient subjects. Mammals include white-tailed deer, nine-banded armadillo, raccoon, Virginia opossum, eastern fox squirrel, and gray squirrel. Scan the board inside the entrance building for updated sightings of birds and other wildlife. Check out the books and other items for sale

White-striped Longtail

RAB/Naturewide Images

and, during winter, inquire about bird walks and nocturnal prowls.

Brazos Bend boasts its own Fourth of July butterfly count. Visitors whose hit lists include Western Pygmy Blue, or southern strays such as White-striped Longtail, Ceraunus Blue, or Great Purple Hairstreak, should check out the Texas Naturalist Web site for count details and for John and Gloria Tveten's complete list of East Texas butterflies.

Nearby Davis Estates Road, much of it unpaved, is favored by local naturalists for its tendency to lure unusual species of birds, butterflies, and dragonflies. To get there from Brazos Bend State Park take Texas Highway 762 north for 2.1 miles. The area is being converted to residential development, however, and its appeal as a birding destination will probably continue to decline. During summer, flocks of Wood Storks have been seen in the shallow ponds bordering the road. After passing through an area with low earthen dikes along both sides of the road, watch for a large, shallow, subsidence lake on the left. Property around the lake is private but may be scoped from the road. Look for Anhinga, various large waders, ducks, Wood Stork, Bald Eagle, swallows, and wintering ducks and geese. Occasionally, Harris's Sparrow joins wintering White-crowned, Lincoln's, and Swamp sparrows in the hedgerows. Sorting through the abundant

wintering Savannahs may produce a Le Conte's or Grasshopper Sparrow.

118: Manor Lake and Eagle Nest Lake

All Seasons
Free, Daily
Rating: 1
FM 1462 to Cow Creek Road (sign may be missing; sign on opposite side of road says Jungman). Take Cow Creek Road/Nash Road S 10 miles to Manor Lake (left) and Eagle Nest Lake (right).

Manor Lake is closed, inaccessible, and invisible from the road. Eagle Nest Lake, however, may be viewed from a couple of small pullouts. It

Upland Sandpiper

FINDING BITTERNS

American Bittern

The Least Bittern is an abundant breeder on the Upper Texas Coast, but it occurs in habitat that is largely accessible only by boat: look for these birds in cattails and *Phragmites* cane beds. They prefer freshwater and brackish marsh and are seen in true saltmarsh only infrequently. Look for places where you can walk or drive to the edge of their habitat. It is difficult to get a good sense of their numbers; however, at sites such as J. D. Murphree Wildlife Management Area (site 29), where they may be viewed by boat, their true abundance can be seen. Shoveler Pond at Anahuac National Wildlife Refuge and the viewing tower at Brazos Bend State Park (sites 49 and 116) are other good places to check. Many people overlook the Least Bittern because they are looking for a Green Heron-sized bird, not appreciating how tiny this species really is. Spring and summer birds are quite vocal; listen for their cuckoo- or dovelike cooing or loud, explosive *cak-cak-cak* calls.

The American Bittern is common on the Upper Texas Coast during winter but difficult to find because of its retiring ways and excellent camouflage. The ease of seeing it and the density of its cover often relate to the flooding and burning regimes at the coastal refuges. In spring their deep, pumping vocalizations make the birds easier to locate.

may not be entered. The pleasant route to these two lakes takes the visitor through grazing land that often contains dozens of wintering Sandhill Cranes. Crested Caracaras are occasionally seen in the fields along County Road 25, and Ferruginous Hawk (rare) has occurred here as well. During spring, watch for Long-billed Curlew and Upland Sandpiper. The extensive roadside marshes draw an impressive diversity of waterbirds including Least Bittern, Yellow-crowned Night-Heron, Purple Gallinule, and Common Moorhen. Bald Eagles nest in the area and often drift over these lakes in search of fish.

Generally there are flocks of various waders, and the lake's waters beyond the weedy wetland may be scanned from here as well. Departing Manor Lake, check graveled County Road 27 to the east. Eastern Bluebirds are often common in the pecan woodlands along this road, and Pileated Woodpeckers may be seen near the river.

119: Varner-Hogg Plantation State Historical Park (now Historic Site)

Migrations
Site fee, 8 A.M. to 5 P.M. Wednesday–Saturday
Contact: (979) 345-4656
Rating: 1
Nash/County Road 25 from Manor Lake S 5.8 miles; TX 35 W 2.0 miles; FM 2852 N 3.2 miles to park.

Stately pecan trees scattered throughout this interesting sixty-six acre historic site attract large populations of Eastern Bluebirds. The woodlands along Varner Creek should be checked during spring migration. Census data collected by Charles Brower has indicated good numbers of migrant birds such as Warbling Vireo and Canada Warbler.

120: Hanson Riverside County Park

Migrations
Free, Daily
Rating: 2
TX 35 into West Columbia; turn left in order to stay on TX 35; go about 1.7 miles to park.

A path near the parking lot leads through the woods to an observation deck along the river. Watch for nesting species such as Red-shouldered Hawk, Mississippi Kite, and Northern Parula.

This can be an excellent migrant trap in spring, from mid-March onward. Watch too for Belted Kingfisher and Carolina Wren.

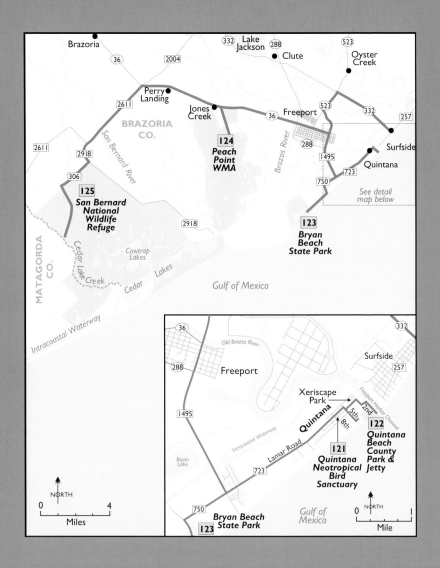

Brazoria

36   2004

Lake
332   Jackson   288   Clute   523
                                                 Oyster
                                                 Creek

Perry
Landing

2611   Jones   Freeport   523   332
                                  Creek   257

BRAZORIA   36
CO.   288
                                                           1495
2611   Surfside

2918   124   750   723   Quintana
306   Peach
                 Point
    125   WMA   See detail
San Bernard   map below
National
Wildlife   2918
Refuge   123

MATAGORDA   Cowtrap   Bryan
CO.   Lakes   Beach
                                                           State Park
              Cedar Lake Creek   Cedar   Lakes

              Intracoastal Waterway   Gulf of Mexico

San Bernard River

Brazos River

NORTH

0   4

    Miles

36   Old Brazos River   332

288   Surfside
         Freeport   257

1495   Xeriscape
                              Park
                                              Freeport Harbor Channel
                                         5th 2nd
                                    Quintana   122
                              723   8th   121   Quintana
    Bryan   Quintana   Beach
    Lake   Intracoastal Waterway   Neotropical County
                              Lamar Road   Bird   Park &
                                               Sanctuary Jetty
750
    Bryan Beach   Gulf of   NORTH
    State Park   Mexico
123   0   1

                                           Mile

San Bernard Loop

This short loop contains five sites that exhibit an ideal array of coastal habitats. It is certainly a worthwhile outing for birders working the Freeport vicinity. More than three hundred species of birds occur here, and visitors on the lookout for unusual birds are often rewarded in this diverse, habitat-rich area. Botanists take note: Nearly one thousand kinds of plants have been recorded here. After wet winters, Texas-sized wildflower displays are diverse, ever changing, and may stretch from horizon to horizon. Photo opportunities abound.

On Quintana Island and the adjoining county park, scan the Gulf's nearshore waters for species such as Northern Gannet, rarities such as Greater Scaup, scoters, or Pomarine Jaeger, and—on very lucky

Brown Pelican

TLE

days—perhaps a Long-tailed Duck or Black-legged Kittiwake. At Bryan Beach, the Brazos River completes its 870-mile journey from North Texas. Its sediment load settles down in the placid Gulf shallows to form sand bars alive with roosting birds such as Black Skimmer, Sandwich Tern, and Brown Pelican. The Quintana Neotropical Bird Sanctuary has produced a steady stream of fall and spring migrants, often in large numbers, as well as rarities such as Yellow-green Vireo. Water drips, wildlife-friendly plantings that attract birds and butterflies, thoughtfully placed benches, and an observation kiosk make this a model sanctuary and conclusively demonstrate that size is no barrier to creating a premier preserve.

San Bernard National Wildlife Refuge and Peach Point Wildlife Management Area make up nearly thirty-eight thousand acres of dry and seasonally flooded woodlands combined with open habitats that include ponds, marshes, and remnants of threatened tall grass coastal prairies. This combination makes these two sites attractive birding venues 365 days a year. Refuge literature indicates that birding is best in winter, when tens of thousands of ducks, geese, Sandhill Cranes, and more than a dozen species of sparrows are present. Visitors from other parts of the country are impressed as well by singing summer residents such as

Orchard Oriole, Painted Bunting, and Dickcissel; by trilling Northern Parula in the huge live oaks; and by refuge ponds that host more than a dozen nesting large waders, King Rail, Purple Gallinule, Boat-tailed Grackle, and plenty of alligators.

121: Quintana Neotropical Bird Sanctuary

All Seasons
Free, Daily
Rating: 3
From the intersection of TX 332 and County Road 257 in Surfside, northwest on TX 332 N 3.7 miles; FM 523 S 1.1 miles; FM 1495 S 1.7 miles; CR 723/Lamar Street E 2.1 miles to sanctuary.

This is one of the great migrant traps on the Upper Texas Coast and, albeit

RAB/Naturewide Images

Western Tanager

of a lesser scale, easily on par with High Island. Surrounded by coastal prairie and marsh, its isolation makes it attractive to migrant landbirds. For birders, the small clumps of salt cedar, small live oaks, lantana, and other low trees and shrubs mean that the birds may be seen at eye level or below. The viewing experience is as intimate as it is excellent. With a six-lot acquisition, the Houston Audubon Society doubled the size of this tiny but critical migrant stopover and placed a conservation easement on the original sanctuary that will protect it for future generations. This site has produced rarities such as Yellow-green Vireo, and the occurrence of Black-whiskered Vireo attracted birders from around the state. Black-throated Blue Warbler occurs from time to time, and locally uncommon birds such as Ladder-backed Woodpecker, Western and Couch's kingbirds, Brown-crested and Ash-throated flycatchers, Bell's Vireo, Black-throated Gray Warbler, Pyrrhuloxia, Western Tanager, Bullock's Oriole, and Lesser Goldfinch show up occasionally. More than the rarities, however, the site's primary appeal is the proximate view that it provides of brilliantly colored warblers, tanagers, and buntings. A dead tree known as "the Snag" should always be checked during migrations.

Xeriscape Park, about a quarter mile from the Neotropical Bird Sanctuary, has thick salt cedar cover for birds, which can be harder to see here than at the sanctuary. Still, some surprises have turned up: Groove-billed Ani, Barn Owl, Long-eared Owl, Townsend's Warbler, and Bobolink.

122: Quintana Beach County Park and Jetty

All Seasons
Site fee, Daily
Rating: 1
From site 121, continue on County Road 723/Lamar Street E 0.2 mile; 5th Street S 0.2 mile to park.

This county park offers typical beach amenities but the Quintana Jetty can also be accessed by a trail past the park, starting from the road leading directly to the jetty. Birding the offshore waters is most productive

Black-legged Kittiwake

when there are trawlers fishing in the vicinity or when incoming boats are discarding fish in the channel. Northern Gannets are frequently seen during winter and spring. Exciting and memorable sightings have been Black-legged Kittiwake, various scoters, Western Grebe, Masked Booby, and Long-tailed Duck.

By scanning the nearshore waters, small numbers of Atlantic bottlenose dolphin can often be seen. This relatively large dolphin reaches a length of about twelve feet and is common close to shore, where it occasionally chases schooling fish right to the water's edge.

This park is the only section of pedestrian-only beach access in the county and provides good habitat and a good viewing experience as a result. The park is manicured and has great amenities for families with its pleasant beach and shaded shelters. Salt cedars right along the dune line can be good for migrants in spring and fall. Other sites nearby are so good that many birders never get as far as the county park, but during migration this site should always be checked. During strong northerly winds in spring and fall, migrant passerines can get blown out over the Gulf at night and then struggle back toward land in the early morning, alighting at the first available perch. It is not unusual

during these episodes to find anomalies such as Cassin's Sparrow out at the end of the jetty. This can be as fascinating as the fallout phenomenon of spring.

From the park, look out toward "Zeus," an old rig that serves as a Peregrine Falcon roost from late fall though early spring. All the migrant traps in the dunes area are home to western diamondback rattlesnakes.

123: Bryan Beach Park (formerly State Park)

All Seasons
Site fee, Daily
Rating: 1
From FM 1495; County Road 750 (Bryan Beach Road) S 0.3 mile to beach; go right, driving on the beach for 3.4 miles to mouth of Brazos River and park entrance.Freeport's Bryan Beach is at the end of FM 1495, just over the state highway bridge at Quintana. Coming off the bridge, go right at the four-way stop sign. The road makes a hard left and hits the beach. When you make the "L" turn, look for a brackish marsh that can be fantastic for terns, shorebirds such as Red Knot, and nesting Snowy Plover. Driving the beach should be avoided except at an extremely low tide, and then only with a four-wheel-drive vehicle.

Red Knot with Long-billed Dowitchers

124: Peach Point Wildlife Management Area Main Unit

Migrations, Winter
Free, Daily
Rating: 2
From FM 1495 and TX 36, take TX 36 N 6.4 miles to wildlife management area.

During late winter and early spring, Barred Owl calls throughout much of the day from the vicinity of the trailhead. Pileated Woodpecker and Northern Parula can be vocal here. The paved, wheelchair-accessible, one-half-mile Live Oak Loop passes through a splendid stand of pictur-

About two miles west of the bridge, look for dredge spoil banks some two hundred yards inland at various points as the beach heads west. In summer there is a rookery with egrets, spoonbills, cormorants, and thousands of shorebirds. Black and Least terns are also abundant.
An open beach with a broad hard-packed sandy area gives way to a track that becomes narrower, and the sand becomes softer. Drive carefully. Driftwood on the beach indicates proximity to the rivermouth. During winter, flocks of Laughing, Herring, Ring-billed, and Bonaparte's gulls can be seen from the beach along with Caspian, Royal, and Forster's terns. Look for Sandwich Tern and Common Tern as well.

Barred Owl

esque trees that beg to be photographed. Many of their branches are
covered with resurrection fern, which
is thick, lush, and green in wetter
seasons. Adjacent Jones Creek Trail
can flood after heavy rain, and after
a wet winter boots may be necessary to traverse the trail successfully.
Cricket frogs chirp from ponds in the
understory, and the drier parts of the
trail are decorated in spring with the
delicate blossoms of false garlic, a
nectar source for the earliest emerg-
ing butterflies.

Totaling 11,938 acres, all very near
sea level, Peach Point WMA should be
one of the most important sites on the
trail, but except for the one-half-mile
paved trail and 2.5 miles of unim-
proved paths that provide access to
oak/hackberry mottes and adjacent
grasslands, Peach Point is off-limits
to the non-hunting public. Expanded
access to the diverse and well-main-
tained habitat would greatly increase
the value of this site to birders. However, the WMA's current goals favor
research and habitat management
over recreational access. There is no
drinking water and there are no rest-
room facilities.

125: San Bernard National Wildlife Refuge

All Seasons
Free, Dawn to Dusk
Rating: 3
From Peach Point continue on TX 36
N 4.6 miles; FM 2611 W 4.3 miles;
FM 2918 1.2 miles; County Road 306
W 1.2 miles to refuge.

This 27,414-acre refuge straddles
Brazoria and Matagorda counties,
twelve miles west of Freeport. After
wet winters it can be boglike until
April or May. Consider rubber boots
for the walk. Visitors should focus on
the Moccasin Pond tour loop, which
is signed on the left. This two-mile
loop has willows along the road that
are great for migrants because there
are no other trees in the area in which
birds can land. Moccasin Pond has
Purple Gallinule and Boat-tailed
Grackle and is excellent for ducks in
winter when water levels are high.
The site also attracts ibis and night-
herons. When water levels begin to
drop the pond can be hopping with
shorebirds. Gull-billed Tern occurs
here as well, and the end of the loop
is good for Eastern Meadowlark,
Crested Caracara, and Savannah
Sparrow (winter).

The Bobcat Woods Trail provides
great opportunities for migrant birds
in spring, dragonflies and butterflies

in summer, and wintering birds in the colder months. Least Flycatcher has occurred here on Christmas bird counts, and the long slough attracts a number of wintering passerines. The boardwalk greatly facilitates viewing. Behind Cocklebur Slough, go to the left, and take the dirt road that crosses over the slough to reach the huge reservoir. This is the best part of the whole refuge. Wolfweed Reservoir can be accessed from the dikes. One side has deeper water; the other side is shallow. In winter huge numbers of waterfowl occur here, and a few Anhinga occur year-round. A walk around the perimeter is essen-

tial. In summer this is one of the few places in the area with fresh water, and in winter Bald Eagle can occur here. Cave Swallow is commonly seen flying over the reservoir. King Rail, Common Moorhen, and coots occur here as well as Neotropic Cormorant. The trees host large numbers of roosting egrets, making this spot a waterbird spectacle for most of the year. The water level determines the occurrence of particular birds. Look in this area for Common Ground-Dove. Farther down the entrance road, Scissortail Trail can be good for *Myiarchus* flycatchers in winter.

FINDING BOAT-TAILED GRACKLES

Boat-tailed Grackle

Although a species of the Gulf Coast, Boat-tailed Grackles live in brackish and freshwater marshes, avoiding true salt marsh. Typically, the dikes at San Bernard, with salt and brackish water on one side and fresh water on the other, are alive with these birds, and during spring and summer their coarse calls, very different from the Great-tailed Grackle's complex vocal repertoire, are perhaps the refuge's most characteristic avian sound. Note that virtually all the grackles on the refuge tour loops are Boat-tailed Grackles. Compared to Great-tailed Grackle, note the Boat-tailed's shorter tail, more rounded forehead, and brown eyes.

Bird Index

Page numbers in *italics* refer to photographs.
Abbreviations following page numbers:

c	call of	br	breeding	f	fall
e	location by ear/sound	ma	massing	sp	spring
h	habitat of	mg	migrating	sm	summer
psh	pisshing/sqeaking	ns	nesting	w	winter
		rst	roosting	yr	year-round

General Index

Page numbers in *italics* refer to photographs.
Abbreviations following page numbers:

c	call of	br	breeding	f	fall
e	location by ear/sound	ma	massing	sp	spring
h	habitat of	mg	migrating	sm	summer
psh	pisshing/sqeaking	ns	nesting	w	winter
		rst	roosting	yr	year-round